Easy

SLOW
COOKER

COOKBOOK

Barbara C. Jones

Published by Cookbook Resources, LLC

D1505722

Easy

Slow Cooker

COOKBOOK

1st Printing   April 2004
Copyright© 2004
By Sheryn R. Jones, Highland Village, Texas.
All rights reserved

ISBN 1-931294-45-3
Library of Congress Number: 2003105100

Illustrations by Nancy Murphy Griffith

Manufactured in China
Edited, Designed and Published in the
United States of America by
Cookbook Resources, LLC
541 Doubletree Drive
Highland Village, Texas 75077
Toll free 866-229-2665
www.cookbookresources.com

cookbook
resources® LLC

This cookbook is dedicated with gratitude and respect to all cooks who bring families to the table for homecooked meals.

Table of

Contents

INTRODUCTION

Born of necessity, these convenient slow cookers make life easier for anyone who uses them. Put your food inside, cover the pot, turn the switch to "on" and come home after hours of errands, soccer games, meetings, work or play and dinner is ready! Meals are simple, convenient and much better than any fast-food, drive-through-window meal.

Easy Slow Cooker Cookbook provides recipes for beef, chicken, seafood, vegetables, soups and casseroles that are great as 1-DISH MEALS or accompaniments with a main dish.

These recipes are family tested and used everyday by moms, dads, seniors, teens and college students. They are packed with nutritious ingredients and are economical, wholesome and practical.

The recipes are easy, simple and everyday cooking that everybody loves. They are ones families grow up on and ones we remember throughout our lives. They are recipes that give us a warm and fuzzy feeling and let us know someone cares about us.

These recipes should never be taken for granted, passed by because they are too simple or too "normal". They are the recipes that strengthen our families and bring us the happiness and satisfaction of being together for a homecooked meal.

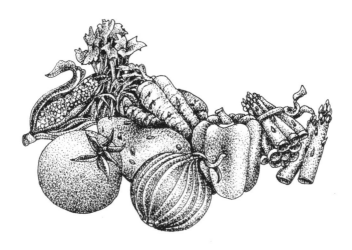

APPETIZERS

Unbelievable Crab Dip

1 (6 ounce) can white crabmeat, drained, picked	1 (170 g)
1 (8 ounce) package cream cheese, softened	1 (227 g)
½ cup (1 stick) butter, sliced	125 mL
2 tablespoons white cooking wine	30 mL

- Combine crabmeat, cream cheese, butter and wine in small slow cooker sprayed with vegetable cooking spray.

- Cover and cook on LOW for 1 hour and gently stir to combine all ingredients.

- Serve from cooker with chips or crackers.

Crab Dip

1 (8 ounce) package cream cheese, softened	1 (228 g)
1 (3 ounce) package cream cheese, softened	1 (85 g)
⅔ cup mayonnaise	160 mL
1 teaspoon seasoned salt	5 mL
1 tablespoon white wine worcestershire sauce	15 mL
1 tablespoon sherry or cooking sherry	15 mL
3 fresh green onions with tops, chopped	3
2 (6 ounce) cans crabmeat, drained, picked	2 (170 g)

- Spray small slow cooker with vegetable cooking spray. In bowl, combine cream cheese, mayonnaise, seasoned salt and worcestershire and mix well with fork.

- Stir in sherry, onions and crabmeat and spoon into slow cooker.

- Cover, cook on LOW for 1½ to 2 hours and stir once.

Broccoli Dip

¾ cup (1½ sticks) butter	175 mL
2 cups thinly sliced celery	500 mL
1 onion, finely chopped	1
3 tablespoons flour	45 mL
1 (10 ounce) can cream of chicken soup	1 (284 g)
1 (10 ounce) box chopped broccoli, thawed	1 (284 g)
1 (5 ounce) garlic cheese roll, cut in chunks	1 (141 g)

- In skillet, melt butter and saute celery and onion, but do not brown; stir in flour.

- Spoon into small slow cooker, stir in remaining ingredients and mix well.

- Cover and cook on LOW for 2 to 3 hours and stir several times.

- Serve with wheat crackers or corn chips.

Cheesy Bacon Dip

2 (8 ounce) packages cream cheese, softened	2 (227 g)
1 (8 ounce) package shredded colby cheese	1 (227 g)
2 tablespoons prepared mustard	30 mL
2 teaspoons white worcestershire sauce	10 mL
4 fresh green onions with tops, sliced	4
¼ to ½ teaspoon salt	2 mL
1 pound bacon, cooked, crumbled	454 g

- Cut cream cheese into cubes and place in 4 or 5-quart (5L) slow cooker.

- Add colby cheese, mustard, white worcestershire, green onions and salt.

- Cover and cook on LOW for 1 hour; stir to melt cheese.

- Stir in crumbled bacon.

- Serve with small-size rye bread or toasted pumpernickel bread.

Hamburger Dip

Men love this meaty, spicy dip.

2 pounds lean ground beef	1 kg
2 tablespoons dry minced onion	30 mL
1½ teaspoons dried oregano leaves	7 mL
1 tablespoon chili powder	15 mL
2 teaspoons sugar	10 mL
1 (10 ounce) can tomatoes and green chilies	1 (284 g)
½ cup chili sauce	125 mL
1 (32 ounce) box Mexican processed cheese, cubed	1 kg

- In large skillet brown ground beef, drain and transfer to 4 or 5-quart (5L) slow cooker sprayed with vegetable cooking spray.

- Add remaining ingredients plus ½ to 1 cup (250 mL) water and stir well.

- Cover, cook on LOW for 1½ to 2 hours. Stir once or twice during cooking time.

- Add a little salt if desired.

- Serve hot with chips or spread on crackers.

Hot Broccoli Dip

1 (16 ounce) box Mexican processed cheese, cubed	1 (454 g)
1 (10 ounce) can golden mushroom soup	1 (284 g)
¼ cup milk	50 mL
1 (10 ounce) box frozen chopped broccoli, thawed	1 (284 g)

- In slow cooker sprayed with vegetable cooking spray, combine cheese, soup and milk, stir well and fold in broccoli.

- Cover and cook on LOW for 1 to 2 hours. Stir before serving.

Chicken-Enchilada Dip

2 pounds boneless, skinless chicken thighs, cubed	1 kg
1 (10 ounce) can enchilada sauce	1 (284 g)
1 (7 ounce) can chopped green chilies, drained	1 (198 g)
1 small onion, finely chopped	1
1 large sweet red bell pepper, finely chopped	1
2 (8 ounce) packages cream cheese, cubed	2 (227 g)
1 (16 ounce) package shredded American cheese	1 (454 g)

- In 4 to 5-quart (5L) slow cooker sprayed with vegetable cooking spray, place chicken thighs, enchilada sauce, green chilies, onion and bell pepper.

- Cover and cook on LOW for 4 to 6 hours.

- Stir in cream cheese and American cheese and cook another 30 minutes. Stir several times during cooking.

- Serve with tortilla chips.

Indian-Corn Dip

1 pound lean ground beef	454 g
1 onion, finely chopped	1
1 (15 ounce) can whole kernel corn, drained	1 (438 g)
1 (16 ounce) jar salsa	1 (454 g)
1 (1 pound) box processed cheese, cubed	1 (454 g)

- In skillet, brown and cook grounded beef on low heat for about 10 minutes and drain.

- Transfer to slow cooker and add onion, corn, salsa and cheese.

- Cover and cook on LOW for 1 hour. Remove lid and stir. Serve with tortilla chips.

Pepperoni Dip

1 (6 ounce) package pepperoni	1 (170 g)
1 bunch fresh green onion, thinly sliced	1
½ sweet red bell pepper, finely chopped	½
1 medium tomato, finely chopped	1
1 (14 ounce) jar pizza sauce	1 (422 g)
1 (12 ounce) package shredded mozzarella cheese	1 (340 g)
1 (8 ounce) package cream cheese, cubed	1 (227 g)

- Chop pepperoni into very small pieces and place in small slow cooker.

- Add green onion, bell pepper, tomato and pizza sauce and stir well.

- Cover and cook on LOW for 2½ to 3½ hours.

- Stir in mozzarella and cream cheese until both cheeses melt.

- Serve with wheat crackers or tortilla chips.

Sausage-Hamburger Dip

1 pound bulk pork sausage	454 g
1 pound lean ground beef	454 g
1 cup hot salsa	250 mL
1 (10 ounce) can cream of mushroom soup	1 (284 g)
1 (10 ounce) can tomatoes and green chilies	1 (284 g)
1 teaspoon garlic powder	5 mL
¾ teaspoon ground oregano	4 mL
1 (32 ounce) box processed cheese, cubed	1 (1 kg)

- In large skillet, brown, cook sausage and ground beef for about 15 minutes and drain.

- Place in 4 to 5-quart (5L) slow cooker sprayed with vegetable cooking spray.

- Add salsa, mushroom soup, tomatoes, green chilies, garlic powder and oregano and stir well. Fold in cheese.

- Cover and cook on LOW for 1 hour or until cheese melts. Stir once during cooking time.

- Serve right from cooker.

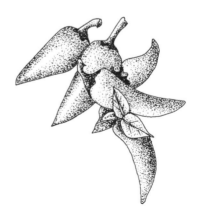

Whiz Bang Dip

1 pound lean ground beef	454 g
1 small onion, very finely chopped	1
1 (2 pound) box processed cheese, cubed	1 (1 kg)
2 (10 ounce) cans chopped tomatoes and green chilies	2 (284 g)
1 teaspoon prepared minced garlic	5 mL

- Brown ground beef and cook on low heat about 10 minutes, breaking up large chunks. Transfer to 4-quart slow cooker.

- Add onion, cheese, tomatoes, green chilies and garlic. Stir well.

- Cover and cook on LOW for 1 hour. Stir to mix well.

- Serve with tortilla chips.

The Big Dipper

2 (15 ounce) cans chili	2 (438 g)
1 (10 ounce) can tomatoes and green chili	1 (284 g)
1 (16 ounce) package cubed processed cheese	1 (454 g)
1 bunch fresh green onions, chopped	1

- Place all ingredients in slow cooker and cook on LOW for 1 to 1½ hours.

- Serve right from slow cooker. Stir before serving.

Firecrackers and Bacon

1 (16 ounce) box Mexican processed cheese, cubed	1 (454 g)
1 (10 ounce) can tomatoes and green chilies	1 (284 g)
1 tablespoon dry minced onion	15 mL
2 teaspoons worcestershire sauce	10 mL
½ teaspoon dried mustard	2 mL
½ cup whipping cream or half-and-half	125 mL
16 slices bacon	16

- Lightly grease small slow cooker and add cubed cheese, tomatoes, green chilies, onion, worcestershire, mustard and cream.

- Turn heat to LOW, cover and cook about 1 hour, stirring several times to make sure cheese melts.

- While cheese melts, place bacon in skillet, fry, drain and crumble.

- Fold three-fourths of bacon into cheese mixture.

- When ready to "dip", sprinkle remaining bacon on top and serve from slow cooker.

Great Balls of Fire

1 pound hot sausage	**454 g**
1 (10 ounce) can chopped tomatoes	**1 (284 g)**
and green chilies	
1 (2 pound) box processed cheese	**1 (1 kg)**

- In skillet, brown sausage, drain and place in small slow cooker sprayed with vegetable cooking spray.

- Stir in chopped tomatoes and green chilies and mix well.

- Cut cheese into chunks and add to sausage-tomato mixture.

- Cover and cook on LOW for 1 hour or until cheese melts.

- Stir when ready to serve and serve hot in slow cooker.

- This works best with large tortilla chips.

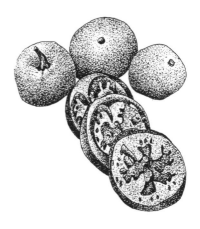

Hot Reuben Spread

1 (8 ounce) package shredded Swiss cheese	1 (227 g)
¾ cup drained sauerkraut, rinsed, drained	175 mL
1 (8 ounce) package cream cheese, softened, cubed	1 (227 g)
2 (2½ ounce) packages sliced corned beef, chopped	2 (70 g)

- Spray small slow cooker with vegetable cooking spray.

- In bowl, combine Swiss cheese, sauerkraut, cream cheese and corned beef and spoon into slow cooker.

- Cover and cook on LOW for 1 hour.

- Serve on slices of 3-inch rye bread.

Crab-Artichoke Spread

1 (6 ounce) can crabmeat, picked	1 (170 g)
½ cup grated parmesan cheese	125 mL
1 bunch fresh green onion, sliced	1
1½ tablespoons lemon juice	22 mL
1 (15 ounce) can artichoke hearts, drained, finely chopped	1 (438 g)
1 (8 ounce) package cream cheese, cubed	1 (227 g)

- In small slow cooker sprayed with vegetable cooking spray, combine all ingredients and stir well.

- Cover and cook on LOW for 1 to 1½ hours. Stir until cream cheese mixes well.

- Serve on toasted bagel chips.

Sausage-Pineapple Bits
The "sweet and hot" makes a delicious combo.

1 (1 pound) link cooked Polish sausage, skinned	1.5 (1 kg)
1 pound hot bulk sausage	454 g
1 (8 ounce) can crushed pineapple, undrained	1 (227 g)
1 cup apricot preserves	250 mL
1 tablespoon white wine worcestershire sauce	15 mL
1½ cups packed brown sugar	375 mL

- Slice link sausage into ½-inch pieces. Shape bulk sausage into 1-inch balls and brown in skillet.

- In slow cooker, place sausage pieces, sausage balls, pineapple, apricot preserves, worcestershire and brown sugar. Stir gently so meatballs do not break up.

- Cover and cook on LOW for 1½ to 2 hours.

Party Smokies

1 cup ketchup	250 mL
1 cup plum jelly	250 mL
1 tablespoon lemon juice	15 mL
2 (5 ounce) packages tiny smoked sausages	2 (141 g)

- Combine all ingredients in small slow cooker.

- Cover and cook on LOW for 1 hour.

- Stir before serving. Serve right from cooker.

Teriyaki Wingettes

2½ pounds wingettes (chicken wings)	1.5 kg
1 onion, chopped	1
1 cup soy sauce	250 mL
1 cup packed brown sugar	250 mL
1 teaspoon minced garlic	5 mL
1½ teaspoons ground ginger	7 mL

- Rinse chicken and pat dry. Place chicken wingettes on broiler pan and broil about 10 minutes on both sides.

- Transfer wingettes to large slow cooker.

- Combine onion, soy sauce, brown sugar, garlic and ginger. Spoon sauce over wingettes.

- Cook on HIGH for 2 hours. Stir wingettes once during cooking to coat chicken evenly with sauce.

Wingettes in Honey Sauce

1 (2 pound) package chicken wingettes	1 (1 kg)
2 cups honey	500 mL
¾ cup soy sauce	175 mL
¾ cup chili sauce	175 mL
¼ cup oil	50 mL
1 teaspoon prepared minced garlic	5 mL

- Rinse chicken, pat dry and sprinkle with salt and pepper.

- Place wingettes on broiler pan and broil for about 20 minutes, 10 minutes on each side or until lightly brown.

- Transfer to slow cooker sprayed with vegetable cooking spray.

- In bowl, combine honey, soy sauce, chili sauce, oil and garlic and spoon over wingettes.

- Cover and cook on LOW for 4 to 5 hours or on HIGH for 2 to 2½ hours. Garnish with dried parsley

Spicy Franks

1 cup packed brown sugar	250 mL
1 cup chili sauce	250 mL
1 tablespoon red wine vinegar	15 mL
2 teaspoons soy sauce	10 mL
2 teaspoons Dijon mustard	10 mL
2 (12 ounce) packages frankfurters	2 (340 g)

- In small slow cooker sprayed with vegetable cooking spray, combine brown sugar, chili sauce, vinegar, soy sauce and mustard and mix well. Cut frankfurters diagonally in 1-inch pieces. Stir in frankfurters.

- Cover and cook on LOW for 1 to 2 hours.

- Serve from cooker using cocktail picks.

Bubbly Franks

1 (1 pound) package wieners	1 (500 g)
½ cup chili sauce	125 mL
⅔ cup packed brown sugar	175 mL
½ cup bourbon	125 mL

- Cut wieners diagonally into bite-size pieces.

- Combine chili sauce, sugar and bourbon in small slow cooker.

- Stir in wieners and cook on LOW for 1 to 2 hours.

- Serve in chafing dish.

SOUPS, STEWS, CHOWDERS & JAMBALAYA

Potato Soup Plus!

5 medium potatoes, peeled, cubed	5
2 cups cooked, cubed ham	500 mL
1 cup fresh broccoli florets, cut very, very fine	250 mL
1 (10 ounce) can cheddar cheese soup	1 (284 g)
1 (10 ounce) can fiesta nacho cheese soup	1 (284 g)
1 (14 ounce) can chicken broth	1 (420 g)
2½ soup cans milk	625 g
Paprika	

- Place potatoes, ham and broccoli in slow cooker sprayed with vegetable cooking spray.

- In saucepan, combine soups and milk. Heat just enough to mix until smooth. Stir into ingredients already in slow cooker.

- Cover and cook on LOW for 7 to 9 hours.

- When serving, sprinkle a little paprika over each serving.

Mexican-Meatball Soup

3 (14 ounce) cans beef broth	3 (422 g)
1 (16 ounce) jar hot salsa	1 (454 g)
1 (16 ounce) package frozen whole kernel corn, thawed	1 (454 g)
1 (16 ounce) package frozen meatballs, thawed	1 (454 g)
1 teaspoon minced garlic	5 mL

- Combine all ingredients in slow cooker and stir well.

- Cover and cook on LOW for 4 to 7 hours.

Tasty Chicken and Rice Soup

1 pound boneless skinless chicken breasts	500 g
½ cup uncooked brown rice	125 mL
1 (10 ounce) can cream of chicken soup	1 (284 g)
1 (10 ounce) can cream of celery soup	1 (284 g)
1 (14 ounce) can chicken broth with roasted garlic	1 (420 g)
1 (16 ounce) package frozen sliced carrots, thawed	1 (454 g)
1 cup half-and-half cream	250 mL

- Cut chicken into 1-inch pieces. Place pieces in sprayed 4 or 5-quart (5 L) slow cooker, sprayed with vegetable cooking spray.

- In bowl, combine and mix rice, both soups, chicken broth and carrots and pour over chicken.

- Cover and cook on LOW 7 to 8 hours.

- Turn heat to HIGH, add half-and-half cream and cook another 15 to 20 minutes.

Taco Soup

1½ pounds lean ground beef	750 g
1 (1 ounce) envelope taco seasoning	1 (28 g)
2 (15 ounce) cans Mexican stewed tomatoes	2 (438 g)
2 (15 ounce) cans chili beans, liquid reserved	2 (438 g)
1 (15 ounce) can whole kernel corn, drained	1 (438 g)
Crushed tortilla chips	
Shredded cheddar cheese	

- In skillet, brown ground beef until it is no longer pink. Place in 5 to 6-quart (6 L) slow cooker.

- Add taco seasoning, tomatoes, chili beans, corn and 1 cup (250 mL) water and mix well.

- Cover and cook on LOW for 4 hours or on HIGH for 1 to 2 hours.

- Serve over crushed tortilla chips and sprinkle some shredded cheddar cheese over top of each serving.

Taco Soup Olé

2 pounds lean ground beef	1 kg
2 (15 ounce) cans ranch-style beans, liquid reserved	2 (438 g)
1 (15 ounce) can whole kernel corn, drained	1 (438 g)
2 (15 ounce) cans stewed tomatoes	2 (438 g)
1 (10 ounce) can tomatoes and green chilies	1 (284 g)
1 (1.3 ounce) envelope ranch dressing mix	1 (32 g)
1 (1 ounce) envelope taco seasoning	1 (28 g)

- In large skillet, brown ground beef, drain and transfer to slow cooker.

- Add remaining ingredients and stir well.

- Cover and cook on LOW for 8 to 10 hours.

Tip: When serving, you might want to sprinkle shredded cheddar cheese over each serving.

Taco-Chili Soup

2 pounds very lean stew meat	1 kg
2 (15 ounce) cans Mexican stewed tomatoes	2 (438 g)
1 (1 ounce) package taco seasoning mix	1 (28 g)
2 (15 ounce) cans pinto beans, liquid reserved	2 (438 g)
1 (15 ounce) can whole kernel corn, liquid reserved	1 (438 g)

- Cut large pieces of stew meat in half and brown in large skillet.

- In 4 or 5-quart (5 L) slow cooker, combine stew meat, tomatoes, taco seasoning mix, beans, corn and 3/4 cup (75 mL) water. (If you are not into "spicy", use original recipe stewed tomatoes instead of Mexican.)

- Cover and cook on LOW for 5 to 7 hours.

Tip: For garnish top each serving with chopped green onions.

Spicy Sausage Soup

1 pound mild bulk sausage	500 g
1 pound hot bulk sausage	500 g
2 (15 ounce) cans Mexican stewed tomatoes	2 (438 g)
3 cups chopped celery	750 ml
1 cup sliced carrots	250 ml
1 (15 ounce) can cut green beans, drained	1 (438 g)
1 (14 ounce) can chicken broth	1 (438 g)
1 teaspoon seasoned salt	5 mL

- Combine mild and hot sausage, shape into small balls and place in non-stick skillet. Brown thoroughly and drain.

- Place in large slow cooker.

- Add all remaining ingredients plus 1 cup (250 ml) water and stir gently so meatballs will not break-up.

- Cover and cook on LOW 6 to 7 hours.

Tortilla Soup

3 large boneless, skinless chicken breast halves, cubed	3
1 (10 ounce) package frozen whole kernel corn, thawed	1 (284 g)
1 onion, chopped	1
3 (14 ounce) cans chicken broth	3 (400 g)
1 (6 ounce) can tomato paste	1 (180 g)
2 (10 ounce) cans tomatoes and green chilies	2 (284 g)
2 teaspoons ground cumin	10 mL
1 teaspoon chili powder	5 mL
1 teaspoon seasoned salt	5 mL
1 teaspoon minced garlic	5 mL
6 corn tortillas	6

- In large slow cooker, combine chicken cubes, corn, onion, broth, tomato paste, tomatoes, green chilies, cumin, chili powder, seasoned salt, garlic and cayenne pepper.

- Cover and cook on LOW for 5 to 7 hours or on HIGH for 3 to 3½ hours.

- While soup is cooking, cut tortillas into ¼-inch (6 mm) strips and place on baking sheet.

- Bake at 375° (190° C) for about 5 minutes or until crisp.

- Serve baked tortilla strips with soup.

Southern Soup

1½ cups dried black-eyed peas	375 mL
2 to 3 cups cooked, cubed ham	500 mL
1 (15 ounce) can whole kernel corn	1 (420 g)
1 (10 ounce) package frozen cut okra, thawed	1 (284 g)
1 onion, chopped	1
1 large potato, cut into small cubes	1
2 teaspoons Cajun seasoning	10 mL
1 (14 ounce) can chicken broth	1 (420 mL)
2 (15 ounce) cans Mexican stewed tomatoes	2 (438 g)

- Rinse peas and drain. In large saucepan, combine peas and 5 cups (4 L plus 250 mL) water.

- Bring to boil, reduce heat, simmer about 10 minutes and drain.

- In 5 or 6-quart (6L) slow cooker, combine peas, ham, corn, okra, onion, potato, seasoning, broth and 2 cups (500 mL) water.

- Cover and cook on LOW for 6 to 8 hours.

- Add stewed tomatoes and continue cooking for 1 more hour.

Saucy Cabbage Soup

1 pound lean ground beef	500 g
1 small head cabbage, chopped	1
2 (15 ounce) cans jalapeno pinto beans, liquid reserved	2 (438 g)
1 (15 ounce) can tomato sauce	1 (438 g)
1 (15 ounce) can Mexican stewed tomatoes	1 (438 g)
1 (14 ounce) can beef broth	1 (420 g)
2 teaspoons ground cumin	10 mL

- In skillet brown ground beef, drain and place in 5 to 6-quart (6 L) slow cooker.

- Add cabbage, beans, tomato sauce, tomatoes, broth, cumin and 1 cup (250 mL) water and mix well.

- Cover and cook on LOW for 5 to 6 hours or until cabbage is tender.

Soup With a Zip

2 (15 ounce) cans Mexican stewed tomatoes	2 (438 g)
2 (14 ounce) cans chicken broth	2 (438 g)
2 (10 ounce) cans chicken noodle soup	2 (284 g)
1 (15 ounce) can shoepeg corn, drained	1 (438 g)
1 (15 ounce) can cut green beans, drained	1 (438 g)
Shredded pepper-jack cheese	

- Place all ingredients in 4 to 5-quart (5 L) slow cooker and mix well.

- Cover and cook on LOW for 2 to 3 hours.

- When ready to serve, sprinkle lots of shredded pepper-jack cheese over each bowl of soup.

Potato and Leek Soup

1 (1.8 ounce) envelope white sauce mix	1 (40 g)
1 (28 ounce) package frozen hash brown potatoes with onion and peppers	1 (800 g)
3 medium leeks, sliced	3
3 cups cooked, cubed ham	750 mL
1 (12 ounce) can evaporated milk	1 (355 g)
1 (8 ounce) carton sour cream	1 (250 g)

- In 4 to 5-quart (5 L) slow cooker, pour 3 cups (750 mL) water, add white sauce and stir until smooth.

- Add hash brown potatoes, leeks, ham and evaporated milk.

- Cover and cook on LOW for 7 to 9 hours or on HIGH for 3½ to 4½ hours.

- When ready to serve, turn heat to HIGH. Take out about 2 cups (500 mL) of hot soup and pour into separate bowl. Stir in sour cream and return to cooker.

- Cover and continue cooking for 15 minutes or until mixture is thoroughly heated.

Pork and Hominy Soup

2 pounds pork shoulder	1 kg
1 onion, chopped	1
2 ribs celery, sliced	1
2 (15 ounce) cans yellow hominy, liquid reserved	1 (438 g)
2 (15 ounce) cans stewed tomatoes	1 (438 g)
2 (14 ounce) cans chicken broth	1 (420 g)
1½ teaspoons ground cumin	7 mL

- Cut pork into ½-inch (13 mm) cubes.

- Sprinkle pork cubes with salt and pepper and brown in skillet.

- Place in 5 to 6-quart (6 L) slow cooker.

- Combine onion, celery, hominy, stewed tomatoes, ground cumin and 1 cup (250 mL) water.

- Pour over pork cubes.

- Cover and cook on HIGH for 6 to 7 hours.

- Serve with warmed, buttered tortillas and top each bowl of soup with some shredded cheese and chopped green onions.

Pizza Soup

3 (10 ounce) cans tomato bisque soup	3 (284 g)
1 (10 ounce) can French onion soup	1 (284 g)
2 teaspoons Italian seasoning	10 mL
¾ cup uncooked tiny pasta shells	175 mL
1½ cups shredded mozzarella cheese	375 mL

- In 4 to 6-quart (6 L) slow cooker, place 4 cans soup, Italian seasoning and 1½ soup cans (340 mL) water. Turn heat setting to HIGH and cook 1 hour or until mixture is hot.

- Add pasta shells or ditali and cook for 1½ to 2 hours or until pasta is cooked.

- Stir several times to keep pasta from sticking to bottom of slow cooker.

- Turn heat off, add mozzarella cheese and stir until cheese melts.

   Tip: For a special way to serve this soup, sprinkle some french-fried onions over top of each serving.

Pinto Bean-Vegetable Soup

4 (15 ounce) cans seasoned pinto beans, liquid reserved	4 (438 g)
1 (10 ounce) package frozen Seasoning Blend chopped onions and peppers	1 (284 g)
2 cups chopped celery	500 mL
2 (14 ounce) cans chicken broth	2 (420 g)
1 teaspoon Cajun seasoning	5 mL
⅛ teaspoon cayenne pepper	.5 mL

- Place all ingredients plus 1 cup (250 mL) water in 5-quart (5 L) slow cooker and stir well.

- Cover and cook on LOW 5 to 6 hours.

Pasta-Veggie Soup

2 yellow squash, chopped	2
2 zucchini, sliced	2
1 (10 ounce) package frozen whole kernel corn, thawed	1 (284 g)
1 sweet red bell pepper, chopped	1
1 (15 ounce) can stewed tomatoes	1 (438g)
1 teaspoon Italian seasoning	5 mL
2 teaspoons dried oregano	10 mL
2 (14 ounce) cans beef broth	2 (420 g)
¾ cup uncooked small shell pasta	175 mL

- In 6-quart (6 L) slow cooker, combine squash, zucchini, corn, bell pepper, tomatoes, seasonings, beef broth and 2 cups (500 mL) water.

- Cover and cook on LOW for 6 to 7 hours.

- Add pasta shells and cook and additional 30 to 45 minutes or until pasta is tender.

- Garnish with a sprinkle of shredded mozzarella cheese on each bowl of soup.

Navy Bean Soup

8 slices thick-cut bacon, divided	8
3 (15 ounce) cans navy beans, liquid reserved	3 (438 g)
1 carrot	1
3 ribs celery, chopped	3
1 onion, chopped	1
2 (15 ounce) cans chicken broth	2 (438 g)
1 teaspoon Italian seasoning	5 mL
1 (10 ounce) can cream of chicken soup	1 (284 g)

- Cook bacon in skillet, drain and crumble. Reserve about 2 crumbled slices for garnish.

- Cut carrot in half lengthwise and then slice.

- In 5 or 6-quart (6 L) slow cooker, combine beans, carrot, celery, onion, chicken broth, Italian seasoning, 1 cup (250 mL) water and most of crumbled bacon and stir to mix.

- Cover and cook on LOW for 5 to 6 hours.

- Ladle 2 cups (500 mL) soup mixture into food processor or blender and process until smooth.

- Return to cooker, add cream of chicken soup and stir to mix.

- Turn heat to HIGH and cook another 10 to 15 minutes.

Meatball Soup

1 (32 ounce) package frozen meatballs	1 L
2 (15 ounce) cans stewed tomatoes	1 (438 g)
3 large potatoes, peeled, diced	3
4 carrots, peeled, sliced	4
2 medium onions, chopped	2
2 (14 ounce) cans beef broth	2 (420 g)
2 tablespoons cornstarch	30 mL

- In sprayed 6-quart (6 L) slow cooker combine meatballs, tomatoes, potatoes, carrots, onions, beef broth, a little salt and pepper and 1 cup (250 mL) water.

- Cover and cook on LOW for 5 to 6 hours.

- Turn heat to HIGH and combine cornstarch with ¼ cup (50 mL) water. Pour into cooker and cook another 10 or 15 minutes or until slightly thick.

Italian Bean Soup

2 (15 ounce) cans great northern beans, liquid reserved	2 (438 g)
2 (15) ounce) cans pinto beans, liquid reserved	2 (438 g)
1 large onion, chopped	1
1 tablespoon instant beef bouillon	15 mL
1 tablespoon minced garlic	15 mL
2 teaspoons Italian seasoning	10 mL
2 (15 ounce) cans Italian stewed tomatoes	2 (438 g)
1 (15 ounce) can cut green beans, drained	1 (438 g)

- In large slow cooker, combine both cans of beans, onion, beef bouillon, garlic, Italian seasoning and 2 cups (500 mL) water.

- Cover and cook on LOW for 6 to 8 hours.

- Turn heat to HIGH, add stewed tomatoes and green beans and stir well.

- Continue cooking for another 30 minutes or until green beans are tender.

Tip: Serve with crispy Italian toast.

Hamburger Soup

2 pounds lean ground beef	1 kg
2 (15 ounce) cans chili without beans	2 (438 g)
1 (16 ounce) package frozen mixed vegetables, thawed	1 (454 g)
3 (14 ounce) cans beef broth	3 (420 g)
2 (15 ounce) cans stewed tomatoes	2 (438 g)
1 teaspoon seasoned salt	5 mL

- In skillet, brown ground beef until no longer pink. Place in 6-quart (6 L) slow cooker.

- Add chili, mixed vegetables, broth, stewed tomatoes, 1 cup (250 mL) water, seasoned salt and stir well.

- Cover and cook on LOW for 6 to 7 hours.

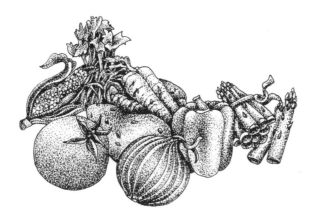

Ham, Bean and Pasta Soup

1 onion, finely chopped	1
2 ribs celery, chopped	2
2 teaspoons minced garlic	10 mL
2 (14 ounce) cans chicken broth	2 (420 g)
2 (15 ounce) cans pork and beans, liquid reserved	2 (438 g)
½ pound ham, cut into 1-inch pieces	250 g
⅓ cup uncooked pasta shells	175 mL

- Cut ham into 1-inch pieces. In 5 or 6-quart (6 L) slow cooker combine onion, celery, garlic, chicken broth, beans, ham and 1 cup (250 mL) water.

- Cover and cook on LOW for 4 to 5 hours.

- Turn cooker to HIGH heat, add pasta and cook another 35 to 45 minutes or until pasta is tender.

- Garnish each serving with cooked crisp and crumbled bacon.

French Onion Soup

5 to 6 sweet onions, thinly sliced	5 to 6
1 clove garlic, minced	1
2 tablespoons (¼ stick) butter	30 mL
2 (14 ounce) cans beef broth	2 (420 g)
2 teaspoons worcestershire sauce	10 mL
6 to 8 (1-inch) slices French bread	6 to 8
8 slices Swiss cheese	8

- In large skillet, cook onions and garlic on low heat (DO NOT BROWN) in hot butter for about 20 minutes and stir several times.

- Transfer onion mixture to 4 to 5-quart (5 L) slow cooker. Add beef broth, worcestershire and 1 cup (250 mL) water.

- Cover and cook on LOW for 5 to 8 hours or on HIGH for 2½ to 4 hours.

- Before serving soup, toast bread slices with cheese slice on top. Broil for 3 to 4 minutes or until cheese is light brown and bubbly.

- Ladle soup into bowls and top with toast.

Tortellini Soup

1 (1.3 ounces) envelope white sauce mix	1 (32 g)
1 (14 ounce) can chicken broth	1 (420 g)
3 boneless, skinless chicken breasts	3
1 teaspoon minced garlic	5 mL
½ teaspoon salt	2 mL
½ teaspoon dried basil	2 mL
½ teaspoon oregano	2 mL
½ teaspoon cayenne pepper	2 mL
1 (8 ounce) package cheese tortellini	1 (250 g)
1½ cups half-and-half cream	1 (375 mL)
6 cups fresh baby spinach	5 L plus
	250 g

- Spray 5 to 6-quart (6 L) slow cooker with vegetable cooking spray and place white sauce mix in cooker.

- Stir in 4 cups (1 L) water and stir gradually until mixture is smooth.

- Cut chicken into 1-inch pieces. Add broth, chicken, garlic, salt, basil, oregano and red pepper to mixture.

- Cover and cook on LOW for 6 to 7 hours or on HIGH for 3 hours.

- Stir in tortellini, cover and cook 1 hour more on HIGH.

- Stir in cream and fresh spinach and cook just enough for soup to get hot .

*Tip: Sprinkle a little shredded parmesan cheese
on top of each serving.*

Enchilada Soup

1 pound lean ground beef, browned, drained	500g
1 (15 ounce) can Mexican stewed tomatoes	1 (438 g)
1 (15 ounce) can pinto beans, liquid reserved	1 (438 g)
1 (15 ounce) can whole kernel corn, liquid reserved	1 (438 g)
1 onion, chopped	1
2 (10 ounce) cans enchilada sauce	2 (284 g)
1 (8 ounce) package shredded 4-cheese blend	1 (227 g)

- Spray 5 to 6-quart (6L) slow cooker with vegetable cooking spray.

- Combine beef, tomatoes, beans, corn, onion, enchilada sauce and 1 cup (250 mL) water and mix well.

- Cover and cook on LOW for 6 to 8 hours or on HIGH for 3 to 4 hours.

- Stir in shredded cheese or hot processed cheese.

- If desired, top each serving with a few crushed tortilla chips.

Delicious Broccoli-Cheese Soup

1 (16 ounce) package frozen chopped broccoli, thawed	1 (454 g)
1 (12 ounce) package cubed processed cheese	1 (340 g)
1 (1.8 ounce) envelope white sauce mix	1 (36 g)
1 (1.3 ounce) envelope dry vegetable soup mix	1 (32 g)
1 (12 ounce) can evaporated milk	1 (340 g)
1 (14 ounce) can chicken broth	1 (420 g)

- In large slow cooker sprayed with vegetable cooking spray, combine all ingredients plus 2 cups (500 mL) water and stir well.

- Cover and cook on LOW for 6 to 7 hours or on HIGH for 3½ to 4 hours.

- Stir about 1 hour before serving time.

Tasty Black Bean Soup

1 pound hot sausage	500 g
1 onion, chopped	1
2 (14 ounce) cans chicken broth	2 (420 g)
2 (15 ounce) cans Mexican stewed tomatoes	2 (438 g)
1 green bell pepper, chopped	1
2 (15 ounce) cans black beans, rinsed, drained	2 (438 g)

- In large skillet, break up sausage and brown with onion. Drain off fat and place in large slow cooker.

- Add chicken broth, stewed tomatoes, bell pepper, black beans and 1 cup (250 mL) water.

- Cover and cook on LOW for 3 to 5 hours.

Sausage-Pizza Soup

1 (16 ounce) package Italian link sausage, thinly sliced	1 (454 g)
1 onion, chopped	1
2 (4 ounce) cans sliced mushrooms	2 (125 g)
1 small sweet green bell pepper, julienned	1
1 (15 ounce) can Italian stewed tomatoes	1 (438 g)
1 (14 ounce) can beef broth	1 (420 g)
1 (8 ounce) can pizza sauce	1 (250 g)
Shredded mozzarella cheese	

- Combine all ingredients in slow cooker and stir well.

- Cover and cook on LOW for 4 to 5 hours.

- Sprinkle mozzarella cheese over each serving.

Creamy Vegetable Soup

3 (14 ounce) cans chicken broth	3 (420 g)
¼ cup (½ stick) butter, melted	50 mL
1 (16 ounce) package frozen mixed vegetables	1 (454 g)
1 onion, chopped	1
3 ribs celery, sliced	3
1 teaspoon ground cumin	5 mL
1 teaspoon salt	5 mL
1 teaspoon black pepper	5 mL
3 zucchini, coarsely chopped	3
2 cups fresh, chopped broccoli	500 mL
1 cup half-and-half cream	250 mL

- In large slow cooker, combine broth, butter, mixed vegetables, onion, celery and seasonings and stir well.

- Cover and cook on LOW for 6 to 7 hours or on HIGH for 3 to 4 hours.

- Stir in zucchini and broccoli. If not using HIGH temperature, turn heat to HIGH and cook another 30 minutes to 1 hour or until broccoli is tender-crisp.

- Turn off heat and stir in half-and-half. Let stand about 10 minutes before serving.

Cream of Zucchini Soup

1 small onion, very finely chopped	1
3½ to 4 cups unpeeled, grated zucchini	850 mL
2 (14 ounce) cans chicken broth	2 (420 g)
1 teaspoon seasoned salt	5 mL
1 teaspoon dried dillweed	5 mL
½ teaspoon white pepper	2 mL
2 tablespoons (¼ stick) butter, melted	30 mL
1 (8 ounce) carton sour cream	1 (250 g)

- In small slow cooker sprayed with vegetable cooking spray, combine all ingredients except sour cream.

- Cover and cook on LOW for 2 hours.

- Fold in sour cream and continue cooking for about 10 minutes or just until soup is hot.

Black Bean Soup

2 (14 ounce) cans chicken broth	2 (420 g)
3 (15 ounce) cans black beans, rinsed, drained	3 (438 g)
2 (10 ounce) cans tomatoes and green chilies	2 (284 g)
1 onion, chopped	1
1 teaspoon ground cumin	5 mL
½ teaspoon dried thyme	2 mL
½ teaspoon dried oregano	2 mL
2 to 3 cups finely diced, cooked ham	500 to 750 mL

- In slow cooker, combine chicken broth and black beans and turn cooker to HIGH .

- Cook just long enough for ingredients to get hot.

- With potato masher, mash about half of the beans in cooker.

- Reduce heat to LOW and add tomatoes, green chilies, onion, spices, diced ham and ¾ cup (175 mL) water.

- Cover and cook for 5 to 6 hours.

Confetti-Chicken Soup

1 pound skinless, boneless chicken thighs	500 g
1 (6.2 ounce) package chicken and herb-flavored rice	1 (180 g)
3 (14 ounce) cans chicken broth	3 (400 g)
3 carrots, sliced	3
1 (10 ounce) can cream of chicken soup	1 (284 g)
1½ tablespoons chicken seasoning	22 mL
1 (10 ounce) package frozen whole kernel corn, thawed	1 (284 g)
1 (10 ounce) package frozen baby green peas, thawed	1 (284 g)

- Cut thighs in thin strips.

- In 5 or 6-quart (6 L) slow cooker, combine chicken, rice, chicken broth, carrots, chicken seasoning and 1 cup (250 mL) water.

- Cover and cook on LOW for 8 to 9 hours.

- About 30 minutes before serving, turn heat to HIGH and add corn and peas to cooker. Continue cooking for another 30 minutes.

Turkey and Mushroom Soup
Another great way to use leftover chicken or turkey

2 cups sliced shitake mushrooms	500 mL
2 ribs celery, sliced	2
1 small onion, chopped	1
2 tablespoons butter	30 mL
1 (15 ounce) can sliced carrots	1 (438 g)
2 (14 ounce) cans chicken broth	1 (420 g)
½ cup orzo pasta	125 mL
2 cups cooked, chopped turkey or chicken	500 mL

- In skillet, saute mushrooms, celery and onion in butter.

- Transfer vegetables to slow cooker and add carrots, broth, orzo and turkey. (Do not use smoked turkey.)

- Cover and cook on LOW for 2 to 3 hours or on HIGH for 1 to 2 hours.

Tasty Cabbage and Beef Soup

1 pound lean ground beef	500 g
1 (16 ounce) package cole slaw mix	1 (454 g)
1 (15 ounce) can cut green beans	1 (438 g)
1 (15 ounce) can whole kernel corn	1 (438 g)
2 (15 ounce) cans Italian stewed tomatoes	2 (438 g)
2 (14 ounce) cans beef broth	2 (420 g)

• In skillet, brown ground beef, drain fat and place in large slow cooker.

• Add slaw mix, green beans, corn, tomatoes and beef broth and add salt and pepper to taste.

• Cover and cook on LOW for 7 to 9 hours. Serve with cornbread.

Chili Soup

3 (15 ounce) cans chili with beans	3 (438 g)
1 (15 ounce) can whole kernel corn	1 (438 g)
1 (14 ounce) can beef broth	1 (420 g)
2 (15 ounce) cans Mexican stewed tomatoes	2 (438 g)
2 teaspoons ground cumin	10 mL
2 teaspoons chili powder	10 mL

• In 5 to 6-quart (6 L) slow cooker, combine chili, broth, corn, stewed tomatoes, ground cumin, chili powder and 1 cup (250 mL) water. Cover and cook on LOW for 4 to 5 hours.

• Serve with warmed, buttered flour tortillas.

Chicken-Pasta Soup

1½ pounds boneless, skinless chicken thighs, cubed	750 g
1 onion, chopped	1
3 carrots, sliced	3
½ cup halved pitted ripe olives	125 mL
1 teaspoon prepared minced garlic	5 mL
3 (14 ounce) cans chicken broth	3 (420 g)
1 (15 ounce) can Italian stewed tomatoes	1 (438 g)
1 teaspoon Italian seasoning	5 mL
½ cup uncooked small shell pasta	125 mL
Parmesan cheese	

- In slow cooker, combine all ingredients except shell pasta and parmesan cheese.

- Cover and cook on LOW for 8 to 9 hours. About 30 minutes before serving, add pasta and stir.

- Increase heat to HIGH and cook another 20 to 30 minutes.

- Garnish with Parmesan cheese.

Chicken and Rice Soup

1 (6 ounce) package long grain and wild rice mix	1 (180 g)
1 (1.3 ounce) envelope chicken noodle soup mix	1 (32 g)
2 (10 ounce) cans cream of chicken soup	2 (284 g)
2 ribs celery, chopped	2
1 to 2 cups cubed, cooked chicken	250 to 500 mL

- In 5 to 6-quart (6 L) slow cooker, combine rice mix, noodle soup mix, chicken soup, celery, cubed chicken and about 6 cups (1.75 L) water.

- Cover and cook on LOW for 2 to 3 hours.

Chicken and Barley Soup

1½ to 2 pounds boneless, skinless chicken thighs	750 g to 1 kg
1 (16 ounce) package frozen vegetables for stews	1 (450 g)
1 (1.3 ounce) envelope dry vegetable soup mix	1 (32 g)
1¼ cups pearl barley	300 mL
2 (14 ounce) cans chicken broth	2 (420 g)
1 teaspoon white pepper	5 mL
1 teaspoon salt	5 mL

- In large slow cooker sprayed with vegetable cooking spray, combine all ingredients and 4 cups (1 L) water.

- Cover and cook on LOW for 5 to 6 hours or on HIGH for 3 hours.

Vegetable-Lentil Soup

2 (19 ounce) cans lentil home-style soup	2 (540 g)
1 (15 ounce) can stewed tomatoes	1 (438 g)
1 (14 ounce) can chicken broth	1 (420 g)
1 onion, chopped	1
1 green bell pepper, chopped	1
3 ribs celery, sliced	3
1 carrot, cut lengthwise in half, sliced	1
2 teaspoons prepared minced garlic	10 mL
1 teaspoon dried marjoram leaves	5 mL

- Combine all ingredients in slow cooker and stir well.

- Cover and cook on LOW for 5 to 6 hours.

Turkey-Tortilla Soup

This is great for leftover turkey.

2 (14 ounce) cans chicken broth	2 (420 g)
2 (15 ounce) cans Mexican stewed tomatoes	2 (438 g)
1 (16 ounce) package frozen succotash, thawed	1 (454 g)
2 teaspoons chili powder	10 mL
1 teaspoon dried cilantro	5 mL
2 cups crushed tortilla chips, divided	500 mL
2½ cups cooked, chopped leftover turkey	625 mL

- In large slow cooker, combine broth, tomatoes, succotash, chili powder, cilantro, ⅓ cup (75 mL) crushed tortilla chips and turkey or chicken and stir well.

- Cover and cook on LOW for 3 to 5 hours.

- When ready to serve, sprinkle remaining chips over each serving.

TIP: Do not use smoked turkey.

Cheesy Potato Soup

6 medium potatoes, peeled, cubed	6
1 onion, very finely chopped	1
2 (14 ounce) cans chicken broth	2 (420 g)
½ teaspoon white pepper	2 mL
1 (8 ounce) package shredded American cheese	1 (225 g)
1 cup half-and-half cream	250 mL

- In slow cooker, combine potatoes, onion, chicken broth and white pepper.

- Cover and cook on LOW for 8 to 10 hours. With potato masher, mash potatoes in slow cooker.

- About 1 hour before serving, stir in cheese and cream and cook 1 more hour.

Cheddar Soup Plus

2 cups milk	**500 mL**
1 (7.06) package cheddar-broccoli soup starter	**1 (220 g)**
1 cup finely chopped, cooked chicken breasts	**250 mL**
1 (10 ounce) package frozen green peas, thawed	**1 (284 g)**
Shredded cheddar cheese	

- Place 5 cups (1.25 L) water and 2 cups (500 mL) milk in slow cooker. Set heat on HIGH until water and milk come to boil.

- Stir contents of soup starter into hot water and milk and stir well. Add chopped chicken, green peas and a little salt and pepper.

- Cook on LOW for 2 to 3 hours.

- To serve, sprinkle cheddar cheese over each serving of soup.

Cajun Bean Soup

1 (20 ounce) package Cajun-flavored, 16-bean soup mix with flavor packet	1 (570 g)
2 cups finely chopped, cooked ham	500 mL
1 chopped onion	1
2 (15 ounce) cans stewed tomatoes	2 (438 g)

- Soak beans overnight in large slow cooker. After soaking, drain water and cover with 2 inches water over beans.

- Cover and cook on LOW for 5 to 6 hours or until beans are tender.

- Add ham, onion, stewed tomatoes and flavor packet in bean soup mix.

- Cook on HIGH for 30 to 45 minutes.

- Serve with cornbread.

Black-Eyed Pea Soup

5 slices thick-cut bacon, diced	5
1 onion, chopped	1
1 green bell pepper, chopped	1
3 ribs celery, sliced	3
3 (15 ounce) cans jalapeno black-eyed peas, liquid reserved	3 (438 g)
2 (15 ounce) cans stewed tomatoes, liquid reserved	2 (438 g)
1 teaspoon chicken seasoning	5 mL

- In skillet, cook bacon pieces until crisp, drain on paper towel and put in slow cooker.

- With bacon drippings in skillet, saute onion and bell peppers, but do not brown.

- To bacon in slow cooker, add onions, bell pepper, celery, black-eyed peas, stewed tomatoes, 1½ cups (375 mL) water, 1 teaspoon (5 mL) salt and chicken seasoning.

- Cover and cook on LOW for 3 to 4 hours.

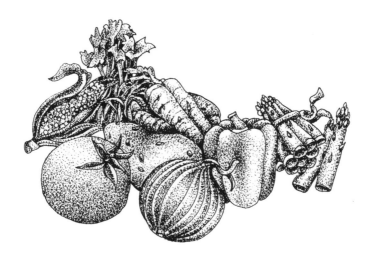

Beefy Rice Soup

1 pound lean beef stew meat	500 g
Seasoned pepper	
1 (14 ounce) can beef broth	1 (420 g)
1 (6.8 ounce) box beef-flavored rice and vermicelli mix	1 (184 g)
1 (10 ounce) package frozen peas and carrots	1 (284 g)
2½ cups vegetable juice	625 mL

- Sprinkle stew meat with seasoned pepper, brown in non-stick skillet, drain and place in large slow cooker.

- Add broth, rice and vermicelli mix, peas, carrots, vegetable juice and 2 cups (500 mL) water.

- Cover and cook on LOW for 6 to 7 hours.

Beef and Black Bean Soup

1 pound lean ground beef	500 g
2 onions, chopped	2
2 cups sliced celery	500 mL
2 (14 ounce) cans beef broth	2 (420 g)
1 (15 ounce) can Mexican stewed tomatoes	1 (438 g)
2 (15 ounce) cans black beans, rinsed, drained	2 (438 g)

- In skillet, brown beef until no longer pink. Place in 5 to 6-quart (6 L) slow cooker.

- Add onions, celery, broth, stewed tomatoes, black beans and ¾ cup (175 mL) water plus a little salt and pepper.

- Cover and cook on LOW for 6 to 7 hours or on HIGH for 3 to 3½ hours.

TIP: If you like a zestier soup,
add 1 teaspoon (5 mL) chili powder.

Beef and Noodle Soup

1½ pounds lean ground beef	750 g
1 onion, chopped	1
2 (15 ounce) cans mixed vegetables, drained	2 (438 g)
2 (15 ounce) cans Italian stewed tomatoes	2 (438 g)
2 (14 ounce) cans beef broth	2 (420 g)
1 teaspoon dried oregano	5 mL
1 cup uncooked medium egg noodles	250 mL

- In skillet, brown and cook ground beef until no longer pink and transfer to slow cooker.

- Add onion, mixed vegetables, stewed tomatoes, beef broth and oregano.

- Cover and cook on LOW for 4 to 5 hours.

- In saucepan, cook noodles according to package direction. Add noodles to slow cooker and cook 30 minutes.

Beef and Barley Soup

1 pound lean ground beef	500 g
3 (14 ounce) cans beef broth	3 (420 g)
¾ cup quick-cooking barley	175 mL
3 cups sliced carrots	750 mL
2 cups sliced celery	500 mL
2 teaspoons beef seasoning	10 mL

- In skillet, brown ground beef, drain and transfer to 5-quart (5 L) slow cooker.

- Add beef broth, barley, carrots, celery and beef seasoning.

- Cover and cook on LOW 7 to 8 hours.

Beans and Sausage Soup

1 pound hot Italian sausage	500 g
1 onion, chopped	1
1 (15 ounce) can Italian stewed tomatoes	1 (438 g)
2 (5 ounce) cans black beans, rinsed, drained	2 (140 g)
2 (15 ounce) cans navy beans, liquid reserved	2 (438 g)
2 (14 ounce) cans beef broth	2 (420 g)
1 teaspoon minced garlic	5 mL
1 teaspoon dried basil	5 mL

- Cut sausage into ½-inch pieces. In skillet, brown Italian sausage and onion, drain and transfer to 5 to 6-quart (6 L) slow cooker.

- Stir in stewed tomatoes, black beans, navy beans, beef broth, garlic and basil and mix well.

- Cover and cook on LOW for 5 to 7 hours.

Beans and Barley Soup

2 (15 ounce) cans pinto beans, liquid reserved	2 (438 g)
3 (14 ounce) cans chicken broth	3 (420 g)
½ cup quick-cooking barley	125 mL
1 (15 ounce) can Italian stewed tomatoes	1 (438 g)
½ teaspoon black pepper	2 mL

- In 6-quart (6 L) slow cooker, combine beans, broth, barley, stewed tomatoes and black pepper and stir well.

- Cover and cook on LOW for 4 to 5 hours.

Minestrone Soup

2 (15 ounce) cans Italian stewed tomatoes	2 (438 g)
2 (16 ounce) packages frozen vegetables and pasta-seasoned sauce	2 (450 g)
3 (14 ounce) cans beef broth	3 (400 g)
2 stalks celery, chopped	2
2 potatoes, peeled, cut into small chunks	2
1 teaspoon Italian seasoning	5 mL
2 (15 ounce) cans kidney beans, drained, rinsed	2 (438 g)
2 teaspoons minced garlic	10 mL

- In large sprayed slow cooker, combine tomatoes, vegetables, broth, celery, potatoes, Italian seasoning, kidney beans, garlic and 1 cup (250 mL) water and mix well.

- Cover and cook on LOW for 4 to 6 hours.

Winter Minestrone

1 pound uncooked Italian sausage links	500 g
2½ cups butternut or acorn squash	625 mL
2 medium potatoes, peeled	2
2 medium fennel bulbs, trimmed	2
1 onion, chopped	1
1 (15 ounce) can kidney beans, rinsed, drained	1 (438 g)
2 teaspoons prepared minced garlic	10 mL
1 teaspoon Italian seasoning	5 mL
2 (14 ounce) cans chicken broth	2 (420 g)
1 cup dry white wine	250 mL
3 to 4 cups fresh spinach	750 mL to 1 L

- Cut sausage, potatoes and fennel into ½-inch slices.

- In skillet cook sausage until brown and drain.

- In large slow cooker, combine squash, potatoes, fennel, onion, beans, garlic and Italian seasoning.

- Top with sausage and pour chicken broth and wine over all.

- Cover and cook on LOW for 7 to 9 hours.

- Stir in spinach, cover and cook 10 more minutes.

Pancho Villa Stew

3 cups diced, cooked ham	750 mL
1 pound smoked sausage	500 g
3 (14 ounce) cans chicken broth	3 (420 g)
1 (15 ounce) can diced tomatoes	1 (438 g)
1 (7 ounce) can chopped green chilies	1 (200 g)
1 onion, chopped	1
2 (15 ounce) cans pinto beans, liquid reserved	2 (438 g)
1 (15 ounce) can whole kernel corn	2 (438 g)
1 teaspoon garlic powder	5 mL
2 teaspoons ground cumin	10 mL
2 teaspoons cocoa	10 mL
1 teaspoon salt	5 mL
1 teaspoon dried oregano	5 mL

- Cut sausage into ½-inch pieces.

- In slow cooker, combine all ingredients and stir well.

- Cover and cook on LOW for 5 to 7 hours.

- Serve with buttered flour tortillas.

Chicken-Tortellini Stew

1 (9 ounce) package cheese-filled tortellini	1 (250 g)
2 small to medium yellow squash, halved, sliced	2
1 sweet red bell pepper, coarsely chopped	1
1 onion, chopped	1
2 (14 ounce) cans chicken broth	2 (420 g)
1 teaspoon dried rosemary	5 mL
½ teaspoon dried basil	2 mL
2 cups cooked, chopped chicken	500 mL

- Place tortellini, squash, bell pepper and onion in slow cooker.

- Stir in broth, rosemary, basil and chicken.

- Cover and cook on LOW for 2 to 4 hours or until tortellini and vegetables are tender.

A Different Stew

2 pounds premium lean beef stew meat	1 kg
½ teaspoon black pepper	2 mL
1 (16 ounce) package frozen Oriental stir-fry vegetables, thawed	1 (450 g)
1 (10 ounce) can beefy mushroom soup	1 (284 g)
1 (10 ounce) can beef consomme	1 (284 g)
⅔ cup bottled sweet and sour sauce	150 mL
1 tablespoon beef seasoning	15 mL

- In skillet brown stew meat sprinkled with some black pepper and place in slow cooker.

- In bowl, combine vegetables, soup, consomme, sweet and sour sauce, beef seasoning and 1 cup (250 mL) water. Pour over stew meat and stir well.

- Cover and cook on LOW for 5 to 7 hours.

Southern Ham Stew

This is great served with cornbread.

2 cups dried black-eyed peas	500 mL
3 cups cooked, cubed ham	750 mL
1 large onion, chopped	1
2 cups sliced celery	500 mL
1 (15 ounce) can yellow hominy, drained	1 (438 g)
2 (15 ounce) cans stewed tomatoes	2 (438 g)
1 (10 ounce) can chicken broth	1 (284 g)
2 teaspoons seasoned salt	10 mL
2 tablespoons cornstarch	30 mL

- Rinse and drain dried black-eyed peas in saucepan. Cover peas with water, bring to boil and drain again.

- Place peas in large slow cooker and add 5 cups (1.25 L) water, ham, onion, celery, hominy, tomatoes, broth and seasoned salt.

- Cover and cook on LOW for 7 to 9 hours.

- Mix cornstarch with about ⅓ cup (75 mL) water, turn cooker to HIGH heat, pour in cornstarch mixture and stir well.

- Cook just about 10 minutes or until stew thickens. Add good amount of salt and pepper and stir well before serving.

TIP: If you would like a little spice in the stew, substitute one of the cans of stewed tomatoes for the Mexican stewed tomatoes.

Serious Bean Stew

1 (16 ounce) package smoked sausage links	1 (454 g)
1 (28 ounce) can baked beans, liquid reserved	1 (800 g)
1 (15 ounce) can great northern beans, liquid reserved	1 (438 g)
1 (15 ounce) can pinto beans, liquid reserved	1 (438 g)
1 (15 ounce) can lentil soup	1 (438 g)
1 onion, chopped	1
1 teaspoon Cajun seasoning	5 mL
2 (15 ounce) cans stewed tomatoes	2 (438 g)

- Peel skin from sausage links and slice.

- Place in 6-quart (6 L) slow cooker, add all remaining ingredients and stir to mix.

- Cover and cook on LOW for 3 to 4 hours.

- Serve with corn muffins.

Santa Fe Stew
A hearty, filling soup

1½ pounds lean ground beef	750 g
1 (14 ounce) can beef broth	1 (420 g)
1 (15 ounce) can whole kernel corn, liquid reserved	1 (438 g)
2 (15 ounce) cans pinto beans, liquid reserved	2 (438 g)
2 (15 ounce) cans Mexican stewed tomatoes	2 (438 g)
1 tablespoon beef seasoning	15 mL
1 (16 ounce) box processed cheese, cubed	1 (454 g)

- In skillet, brown beef until no longer pink.

- Place in 5 to 6-quart (6 L) slow cooker and add broth, corn, beans, stewed tomatoes and beef seasoning.

- Cook on LOW for 5 to 6 hours.

- When ready to serve, fold in cheese chunks and stir until cheese melts.

TIP: Cornbread is a must to serve with this stew.

Roast and Vegetable Stew

3 cups leftover roast beef, cubed	750 mL
2 (15 ounce) cans stewed tomatoes	2 (438 g)
1 (16 ounce) package frozen mixed vegetables, thawed	1 (450 g)
2 (14 ounce) cans beef broth	2 (420 g)
1 cup cauliflower florets, optional	250 mL
1 cup broccoli florets, optional	250 mL

- Combine all ingredients except cauliflower and broccoli in 6-quart (6 L) slow cooker. Add salt and pepper.

- Cover and cook on LOW for 5 to 7 hours.

- About 2 hours before serving, stir in cauliflower and broccoli and continue cooking until tender.

Pork-Vegetable Stew

1 pork tenderloin	1
1 onion, coarsely chopped	1
1 sweet red bell pepper, julienned	1
1 (16 ounce) package frozen mixed vegetables, thawed	1 (454 g)
2 tablespoons flour	30 mL
1 (10 ounce) can chicken broth	1 (284 g)
½ teaspoon dried rosemary leaves	2 mL
½ teaspoon oregano leaves	2 mL
1 (6 ounce) package long-grain, wild rice	1 (180 g)

- Cut tenderloin into 1-inch cubes. In non-stick skillet, brown tenderloin cubes and place in large slow cooker sprayed with vegetable cooking spray.

- Add onion, bell pepper and mixed vegetables.

- In bowl, stir flour, rosemary and oregano into chicken broth and pour over vegetables.

- Cover and cook on LOW for 4 to 4½ hours.

- When ready to serve, cook rice according to package directions.

- Serve pork and vegetables over rice.

Olé! For Stew

1½ to 2 pounds lean beef stew meat	750 mL to 1 kg
2 (15 ounce) cans pinto beans, undrained	2 (438 g)
1 onion, chopped	1
3 carrots, sliced	3
2 medium potatoes, cubed	2
1 (1.3 ounce) envelope taco seasoning	1 (32 g)
2 (15 ounce) cans Mexican stewed tomatoes	2 (438 g)

- In non-stick skillet, brown stew meat.

- In large slow cooker, combine stew meat, pinto beans, onion, carrots, potatoes, taco seasoning and 2 cups (500 mL) water.

- Cover and cook on LOW for 6 to 7 hours.

- Add stewed tomatoes and cook 1 more hour.

TIP: This is great served with warmed, buttered flour tortillas.

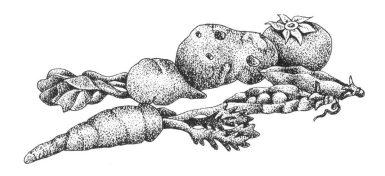

Meatball Stew

1 (18 ounce) package frozen prepared Italian meatballs, thawed	1 (520 g)
1 (14 ounce) can beef broth	1 (420 g)
1 (15 ounce) can cut green beans	1 (438 g)
1 (16 ounce) package baby carrots	1 (454 g)
2 (15 ounce) cans stewed tomatoes	2 (438 g)
1 tablespoon worcestershire sauce	15 mL
½ teaspoon ground allspice	2 mL

- Combine all ingredients in slow cooker.

- Cover and cook on LOW for 3 to 5 hours.

Meatball and Veggie Stew

1 (18 ounce) package frozen cooked meatballs, thawed	1 (520 g)
1 (16 ounce) package frozen mixed vegetables	1 (454 g)
1 (15 ounce) can stewed tomatoes	1 (438 g)
1 (12 ounce) jar beef gravy	1 (340 g)
2 teaspoons crushed dried basil	10 mL
½ teaspoon black pepper	2 mL

- Place meatballs and mixed vegetables in 4 to 5-quart (5 L) slow cooker.

- In bowl stir stewed tomatoes, gravy, basil, black pepper and ½ cup (125 mL) water. Pour over meatballs and vegetables.

- Cover and cook on LOW for 6 to 7 hours.

Italian-Vegetable Stew

1½ to 2 pounds Italian sausage	750 mL to 1 kg
2 (16 ounce) packages frozen vegetables	2 (454 g)
2 (15 ounce) cans Italian stewed tomatoes	2 (438 g)
1 (14 ounce) can beef broth	1 (420 g)
1 teaspoon Italian seasoning	5 mL
½ cup pasta shells	125 mL

- In skillet, brown sausage and cook about 5 minutes and drain.

- In 5 to 6-quart (6 L) slow cooker, combine sausage, vegetables, stewed tomatoes, broth, Italian seasoning and shells and mix well.

- Cover and cook on LOW for 3 to 5 hours.

Hungarian Stew

2 pounds boneless short ribs	1 kg
1 cup pearl barley	250 mL
1 small onion, chopped	1
1 green bell pepper, chopped	1
1 teaspoon prepared minced garlic	5 mL
2 (15 ounce) cans kidney beans, drained	2 (438 g)
2 (14 ounce) cans beef broth	2 (420 g)
1 tablespoon paprika	15 mL

- In slow cooker, combine all ingredients plus 1 cup (250 mL) water.

- Cover and cook on LOW for 8 to 9 hours or on HIGH for 4½ to 5 hours.

Hearty Meatball Stew

1 (28 ounce) package frozen meatballs, thawed	1 (800 g)
2 (15 ounce) cans Italian stewed tomatoes	2 (438 g)
2 (14 ounce) cans beef broth	2 (420 g)
2 (15 ounce) cans new potatoes	2 (438 g)
1 (16 ounce) package baby carrots	1 (454 g)
1 tablespoon Step 1 beef seasoning	15 mL

- Place meatballs, stewed tomatoes, beef broth, potatoes, carrots and beef seasoning in 6-quart (6 L) slow cooker.

- Cover and cook on LOW for 6 to 7 hours.

- Serve with corn muffins.

South-of-the-Border Beef Stew

1½ to 2 pounds boneless, beef chuck roast	750 mL to 1 kg
1 green bell pepper	1
2 onions, coarsely chopped	2
2 (15 ounce) cans pinto beans, liquid reserved	2 (438 g)
½ cup uncooked rice	125 mL
1 (14 ounce) can beef broth	1 (420 g)
2 (15 ounce) cans Mexican stewed tomatoes	2 (438 g)
1 cup mild or medium green salsa	250 mL
2 teaspoons ground cumin	10 mL

- Trim fat from beef and cut into 1-inch cubes. Brown in large skillet and place in large slow cooker sprayed with vegetable cooking spray.

- Cut bell pepper into ½-inch slices. Add remaining ingredients plus 1½ cups (375 mL) water and a little salt.

- Cover and cook on LOW for 7 to 8 hours.

- Serve with warm flour tortillas.

Ham and Cabbage Stew

2 (15 ounce) can Italian stewed tomatoes	2 (438 g)
3 cups shredded cabbage	750 mL
1 onion, chopped	1
1 sweet red bell pepper, chopped	1
2 tablespoons (¼ stick) butter, sliced	30 mL
1 (14 ounce) can chicken broth	1 (420 g)
¾ teaspoon seasoned salt	4 mL
¾ teaspoon black pepper	4 mL
3 cups cooked, diced ham	750 mL

- In large slow cooker, combine all ingredients plus 1 cup (250 mL) water and stir to mix well.

- Cover and cook on LOW for 5 to 7 hours.

- Serve with cornbread.

Comfort Stew

1½ pounds select stew meat	750 g
2 (10 ounce) cans French onion soup	2 (284 g)
1 (10 ounce) can cream of onion soup	1 (284 g)
1 (10 ounce) can cream of celery soup	1 (284 g)
1 (16 ounce) package frozen stew vegetables, thawed	1 (450 g)

- Place stew meat in bottom of slow cooker sprayed with vegetable cooking spray.

- Add soups in order given and spread evenly over meat. DO NOT STIR.

- Turn slow cooker to HIGH and cook just long enough for ingredients to get hot.

- Change heat setting to LOW, cover and cook for 7 to 8 hours.

Chicken Stew over Biscuits

2 (1.3 ounces) envelopes chicken gravy mix	2 (32 g)
2 cups sliced celery	500 mL
1 (10 ounce) package frozen sliced carrots	1 (284 g)
1 (10 ounce) package frozen green peas, thawed	1 (284 g)
1 teaspoon dried basil	5 mL
¾ teaspoon salt	4 mL
¾ teaspoon black pepper	4 mL
3 cups cubed, cooked chicken or turkey breasts	750 mL
Buttermilk biscuits	

- In slow cooker, combine gravy mix, 2 cups (500 mL) water, celery, carrots, peas, basil, salt and pepper and cubed chicken.

- Cover and cook on LOW for 6 to 7 hours.

- Serve over baked refrigerated buttermilk biscuits.

TIP: If you like thick stew, mix 2 tablespoons (30 mL) cornstarch with ¼ cup (50 mL) water and stir into chicken mixture. Cook another 30 minutes to thicken.

Chicken Stew

4 large boneless, skinless chicken breasts, cubed	4
3 medium potatoes, peeled, cubed	3
1 (26 ounce) jar meatless spaghetti sauce	1 (750 g)
1 (15 ounce) can cut green beans, drained	1 (438 g)
1 (15 ounce) can whole kernel corn	1 (438 g)
1 tablespoon chicken seasoning	15 mL

- Combine cubed chicken, potatoes, spaghetti sauce, green beans, corn, chicken seasoning and ¾ cup (175 g) water in 5 to 6-quart (6 L) slow cooker.

- Cover and cook on LOW for 6 to 7 hours.

White Lightning Chili

3 (15 ounce) cans navy beans, liquid reserved	3 (438 g)
3 (14 ounce) cans chicken broth	3 (420 g)
1 (10 ounce) can cream of chicken soup	1 (284 g)
2 tablespoons (¼ stick) butter, melted	30 mL
2 onions, chopped	2
3 cups cooked, chopped chicken or turkey	750 mL
1 (7 ounce) can chopped green chilies	1 (180 g)
1 teaspoon prepared minced garlic	5 mL
½ teaspoon dried basil	2 mL
½ teaspoon white pepper	2 mL
⅛ teaspoon cayenne pepper	.5 mL
⅛ teaspoon ground cloves	.5 mL
1 teaspoon ground oregano	5 mL
1 (8 ounce) package shredded 4-cheese blend	1 (225 g)

- In slow cooker, combine all ingredients except cheese.

- Cover and cook on LOW for 4 to 5 hours.

- When serving, sprinkle cheese over top of each serving.

Vegetarian Chili

2 (15 ounce) cans stewed tomatoes	2 (438 g)
1 (15 ounce) can kidney beans, rinsed, drained	1 (438 g)
1 (15 ounce) can pinto beans, liquid reserved	1 (438 g)
1 onion, chopped	1
1 green bell pepper, chopped	1
1 tablespoon chili powder	15 mL
1 (7 ounce) package elbow macaroni	1 (200 g)
¼ cup (½ stick) butter, sliced	50 mL

- In 4 or 5-quart (5 L) slow cooker, combine tomatoes, kidney beans and pinto beans, onion, bell pepper, chili powder and 1 cup (250 mL) water.

- Cover and cook on LOW for 4 to 5 hours or on HIGH for 2 hours.

- Cook macaroni according to package directions, drain and stir butter into hot macaroni. Fold into chili.

- If desired, top each serving with shredded cheddar cheese.

Vegetable Chili

2 (15 ounce) cans navy beans, liquid reserved	2 (438 g)
2 (15 ounce) cans Mexican stewed tomatoes	2 (438 g)
1 (15 ounce) can pinto beans, liquid reserved	1 (438 g)
1 (15 ounce) can whole kernel corn	1 (438 g)
1 onion, chopped	1
3 ribs celery, sliced	3
1 tablespoon chili powder	15 mL
2 teaspoons dried oregano leaves	10 mL
1 teaspoon seasoned salt	5 mL

- In 5 to 6-quart (6 L) slow cooker, combine both beans, tomatoes, corn, onion, celery, chili powder, oregano, seasoned salt and 1½ cups (375 mL) water.

- Cover and cook on LOW for 4 to 6 hours.

- Serve with hot, buttered broccoli cornbread.

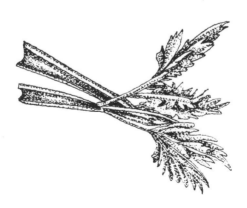

Turkey-Veggie Chili

1 pound ground turkey	500 g
2 (15 ounce) cans pinto beans, liquid reserved	2 (438 g)
1 (15 ounce) can great northern beans, liquid reserved	1 (438 g)
1 (14 ounce) can chicken broth	1 (420 g)
2 (15 ounce) cans Mexican stewed tomatoes	2 (438 g)
1 (8 ounce) can whole kernel corn	1 (225 g)
1 large onion, chopped	1
1 sweet red bell pepper, chopped	1
2 teaspoons prepared minced garlic	10 mL
2 teaspoons ground cumin	10 mL
½ cup uncooked elbow macaroni	125 mL

- In skillet with little oil, cook and brown turkey before adding to large slow cooker.

- Add beans, broth, tomatoes, corn, onion, bell pepper, garlic, cumin and salt to taste and stir well.

- Cover and cook on LOW for 4 to 5 hours.

- Stir in macaroni and continue cooking for about 15 minutes. Stir to make sure macaroni does not stick to cooker and cook another 15 minutes or until macaroni is tender.

TIP: You might want to top each serving with dab of sour cream or 1 tablespoon (15 mL) shredded cheddar cheese.

Traditional Chili

2 pounds lean beef chili meat	1 kg
1 large onion, finely chopped	1
1 (10 ounce) can chopped tomatoes and green chilies	1 (284 g)
2½ cups tomato juice	625 mL
2 tablespoons chili powder	30 mL
1 tablespoon ground cumin	15 mL
1 tablespoon minced garlic	15 mL
1 (15 ounce) can pinto or kidney beans	1 (438 g)

- In large slow cooker combine chili meat, onion, tomatoes, green chilies, tomato juice, chili powder, cumin, garlic and 1 cup (250 mL) water and mix well.

- Cover and cook on LOW for 7 to 9 hours.

- Add pinto or kidney beans and continue to cook another 30 minutes.

Easy Chili

4 pounds lean ground beef	2 kg
2 (10 ounce) packages hot chili mix	2 (284 g)
1 (6 ounce) can tomato sauce	1 (180 g)
2 (15 ounce) cans stewed tomatoes, liquid reserved	1 (438 g)
2½ teaspoons ground cumin	12 mL
1 teaspoon salt	5 mL

- In large skillet break ground beef into pieces, brown and drain. Use slotted spoon to drain fat and place beef in 5 to 6-quart (6 L) slow cooker.

- Add chili mix, tomato sauce, stewed tomatoes, cumin, salt and 1 cup (250 mL) water.

- Cover and cook on LOW setting for 4 to 5 hours. If you think you can't eat chili without beans, add 2 (15 ounce) 2 (438 g) cans ranch-style beans.

Chunky Chili

2 pounds premium cut stew meat	1 kg
1 onion, chopped	1
2 (15 ounce) cans diced tomatoes	2 (438 g)
2 (15 ounce) cans pinto beans, liquid reserved	2 (438 g)
1½ tablespoons chili powder	22 mL
2 teaspoons ground cumin	10 mL
1 teaspoon ground oregano	5 mL

- If stew meat is in fairly large pieces, cut each piece in half.

- In large skillet, brown stew meat and transfer to large slow cooker.

- Add onion, tomatoes, beans, seasonings and salt to taste.

- Cover and cook on LOW for 6 to 7 hours.

- Sprinkle shredded cheese over each serving.

Split-Pea and Ham Chowder

1 medium potato	1
1 (16 ounce) bag split peas, rinsed	1 (454 g)
1 (11 ounce) can whole kernel corn with red and green peppers	1 (312 g)
1 (14 ounce) can chicken broth	1 (420 g)
2 carrots, sliced	2
2 ribs celery, diagonally sliced	2
1 tablespoon dried onion flakes	15 mL
1 teaspoon dried marjoram leaves	5 mL
1 teaspoon seasoned salt	5 mL

- Cut potato into small cubes and add to slow cooker sprayed with vegetable cooking spray.

- In slow cooker combine all ingredients plus 3 cups (750 mL) water and 1 teaspoon salt.

- Cover and cook on LOW for 6 to 8 hours.

Oyster Chowder

1 small sweet red bell pepper, chopped	1
1 onion, chopped	1
1 (14 ounce) can chicken broth	1 (420 g)
1 medium potato, cubed	1
1 fresh jalapeno pepper, finely chopped	1
8 ounces shucked oysters with liquid	225 g
1 (10 ounce) package frozen whole kernel corn, thawed	1 (284 g)
1 teaspoon dried oregano	5 mL
½ cup heavy cream	125 mL

- Combine all ingredients except cream in slow cooker.

- Cover and cook on LOW for 3 to 4 hours.

- When ready to serve, stir in cream.

Ham-Vegetable Chowder
Great recipe for leftover ham

1 medium potato	1
2 (10 ounce) cans cream of celery soup	2 (284 g)
1 (14 ounce) can chicken broth	1 (420 g)
3 cups finely diced ham	750 mL
1 (15 ounce) can whole kernel corn	1 (438 g)
2 carrots, sliced	2
1 onion, coarsely chopped	1
1 teaspoon dried basil	5 mL
1 teaspoon seasoned salt	5 mL
1 teaspoon white pepper	5 mL
1 (10 ounce) package frozen broccoli florets	1 (284 g)

- Cut potato into 1-inch pieces.

- Combine all ingredients except broccoli florets in large slow cooker.

- Cover and cook on LOW for 5 to 6 hours.

- Add broccoli to cooker and cook 1 hour more.

Crab Chowder

2 small zucchini, thinly sliced	2
1 sweet red bell pepper, julienned	1
2 ribs celery, diagonally sliced	2
1 medium potato, cubed	1
2 tablespoons (¼ stick) butter, melted	30 mL
1 (10 ounce) can chicken broth	1 (284 g)
1 teaspoon seasoned salt	5 mL
2 tablespoons cornstarch	30 mL
3 cups milk	750 mL
2 (6 ounce) cans crabmeat, drained, picked	2 (170 g)
1 (3 ounce) package cream cheese, cut up	1 (85 g)

- Place zucchini, bell pepper, celery, potato, butter, broth and seasoned salt in slow cooker.

- Stir cornstarch into milk, stir and pour into slow cooker.

- Cover and cook on LOW for 3 to 4 hours.

- Turn heat to HIGH, add crabmeat and cream cheese and stir until cream cheese melts.

Country Chicken Chowder

1½ pounds boneless, skinless chicken breast halves	750 g
2 tablespoons butter	30 mL
2 (10 ounce) cans cream of potato soup	2 (284 g)
1 (14 ounce) can chicken broth	1 (420 g)
1 (8 ounce) package frozen whole kernel corn	1 (220 g)
1 onion, sliced	1
2 ribs celery, sliced	2
1 (10 ounce) package frozen peas and carrots, thawed	1 (284 g)
½ teaspoon dried thyme leaves	2 mL
½ cup half-and-half cream	125 mL

- Cut chicken into 1-inch strips.

- In skillet, brown chicken strips in butter and transfer to large slow cooker.

- Add potato soup, broth, corn, onion, celery, peas, carrots and thyme and stir.

- Cover and cook on LOW for 3 to 4 hours or until vegetables are tender.

- Turn off heat, stir in half-and-half and set aside for about 10 minutes before serving.

Corn-Ham Chowder

1 (14 ounce) can chicken broth	1 (420 g)
1 cup whole milk	250 mL
1 (10 ounce) can cream of celery soup	1 (284 g)
1 (15 ounce) can cream-style corn	1 (438 g)
1 (15 ounce) can whole kernel corn	1 (438 g)
½ cup dry potato flakes	125 mL
1 onion, chopped	1
2 to 3 cups chopped, (leftover) cooked ham	500 to 750 mL

- In 6-quart (6 L) slow cooker, combine broth, milk, soup, cream-style corn, whole kernel corn, potato flakes, onion and ham.

- Cover and cook on LOW for 4 to 5 hours.

- When ready to serve, season with salt and black pepper.

Chicken Chowder

3 cups cooked, cubed chicken	750 mL
1 (14 ounce) can chicken broth	1 (420 g)
2 (10 ounce) cans cream of potato soup	2 (284 g)
1 large onion, chopped	1
3 ribs celery, sliced diagonally	3
1 (16 ounce) package frozen whole kernel corn, thawed	1 (454 g)
⅔ cup heavy cream	175 mL

- In 5 to 6-quart (6 L) slow cooker combine chicken, chicken broth, potato soup, onion, celery, corn and ¾ cup (175 mL) water.

- Cover and cook on LOW for 3 to 4 hours.

- Add heavy cream to slow cooker and heat another 15 minutes or until heated thoroughly.

Shrimp and Ham Jambalaya

3 ribs celery, diagonally sliced	3
1 onion, chopped	1
1 red bell pepper, chopped	1
1 green bell pepper, chopped	1
2 (15 ounce) cans stewed tomatoes	2 (438 g)
2 cups cooked, cubed smoked ham	500 mL
½ teaspoon cayenne pepper	2 mL
1 tablespoon dried parsley flakes	15 mL
2 teaspoons prepared minced garlic	30 mL
1 pound uncooked peeled, veined shrimp	500 g

- In slow cooker sprayed with vegetable cooking spray, combine celery, onion, bell peppers, tomatoes, ham, cayenne pepper, parsley flakes, garlic, salt and pepper to taste.

- Cover and cook on LOW for 7 to 8 hours or on HIGH for 3 to 4 hours.

- Stir in shrimp and cook on LOW 1 hour.

- Serve over hot cooked rice.

Shrimp and Sausage Jambalaya

1 pound cooked, smoked sausage links	500 g
1 onion, chopped	1
1 green bell pepper, chopped	1
2 teaspoons minced garlic	2
1 (28 ounce) can diced tomatoes	1 (800 g)
1 tablespoon parsley flakes	15 mL
½ teaspoon dried thyme leaves	2 mL
1 teaspoon Cajun seasoning	5 mL
¼ teaspoon cayenne pepper	1 mL
1 pound uncooked, peeled, veined shrimp	500 g
Hot cooked rice	

- In slow cooker sprayed with vegetable cooking spray, combine all ingredients except shrimp and rice.

- Cover and cook on LOW for 6 to 8 hours or on HIGH for 3 to 4 hours.

- Stir in shrimp and cook on LOW for 1 more hour. Serve over hot, cooked rice.

Shrimp and Chicken Jambalaya

4 chicken breast halves, cubed	4
1 (28 ounce) can diced tomatoes	1 (800 g)
1 onion, chopped	1
1 green bell pepper, chopped	1
1 (14 ounce) can chicken broth	1 (422 g)
½ cup dry white wine	125 mL
2 teaspoons dried oregano	10 mL
2 teaspoons Cajun seasoning	10 mL
½ teaspoon cayenne pepper	2 mL
1 pound cooked, peeled, veined shrimp	500 g
2 cups white rice, cooked	500 mL

- Place all ingredients except shrimp and rice in slow cooker and stir.

- Cover and cook on LOW for 6 to 8 hours.

- Turn heat to HIGH, stir in shrimp and rice and cook another 15 to 20 minutes.

VEGETABLES

Broccoli-Cheese Bake

4 tablespoons (½ stick) butter, melted	60 mL
1 (10 ounce) can cream of mushroom soup	1 (284 g)
1 (10 ounce) can cream of onion soup	1 (284 g)
1 cup instant rice	250 mL
1 (8 ounce) package cubed processed cheese	1 (225 g)
2 (10 ounce) packages frozen chopped broccoli, thawed	2 (284 g)

- Combine all ingredients, plus ½ cup (125 mL) water in slow cooker sprayed with vegetable cooking spray and stir well.

- Cover and cook on HIGH for 2 to 3 hours.

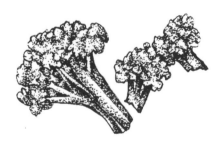

Broccoli and Cheese

2 (16 ounce) packages frozen broccoli florets, thawed	2 (454 g)
2 (15 ounce) cans whole new potatoes, drained	2 (438 g)
2 (10 ounce) cans cream of celery soup	2 (284 g)
½ cup milk	125 mL
1 (8 ounce) package cheddar cheese, divided	1 (225 g)
1½ cups cracker crumbs	375 mL

- Place broccoli on plate and cut off some of stems and discard.

- In slow cooker, combine broccoli and potatoes.

- In saucepan, combine celery soup and milk, heat just enough to mix well and pour over broccoli and potatoes.

- Sprinkle half the cheese and crumbs over broccoli.

- Cover and cook on LOW for 3 to 4 hours.

- When ready to serve, sprinkle on remaining cheese and crumbs on top.

Savory Broccoli and Cauliflower

1 (16 ounce) package frozen broccoli florets, thawed	1 (450 mL)
1 (16 ounce) package frozen cauliflower florets, thawed	1 (450 g)
Salt and pepper to taste	
2 (10 ounce) cans nacho cheese soup	2 (284 g)
6 slices bacon, cooked, crumbled	6

- Place broccoli and cauliflower in slow cooker sprayed with vegetable cooking spray.

- Sprinkle with salt and pepper.

- Spoon soup over top and sprinkle with bacon.

- Cover and cook on LOW for 3 to 4 hours.

Company Broccoli

1½ pounds fresh broccoli, trimmed well	750 g
1 (10 ounce) can cream of chicken soup	1 (284 g)
½ cup mayonnaise	125 mL
1 (8 ounce) package shredded cheddar cheese	1 (228 g)
¼ cup toasted slivered almonds	50 mL

- Place broccoli in slow cooker sprayed with vegetable cooking spray.

- Combine chicken soup, mayonnaise, half the cheese and ¼ cup (50 mL) water. Spoon over broccoli.

- Cover and cook on LOW 2 to 3 hours. When ready to serve, sprinkle remaining cheese over broccoli and top with toasted almonds.

Sunshine Green Beans

2 (16 ounce) packages frozen whole green beans, thawed	2 (454 g)
2 (10 ounce) cans fiesta nacho cheese soup	2 (284 g)
1 (8 ounce) package seasoning blend onions and bell peppers	1 (225 g)
1 (8 ounce) can sliced water chestnuts, cut in half	1 (225 g)
1 teaspoon seasoned salt	5 mL

- Combine all ingredients plus ¼ cup (60 mL) water in large slow cooker and stir to mix well.

- Cover and cook on LOW for 4 to 5 hours.

Southern Green Beans and Potatoes

6 to 8 medium new potatoes, unpeeled, sliced	6 to 8
5 cups fresh whole green beans, trimmed	1.25 L
2 tablespoons dry, minced onions	30 mL
4 tablespoons (½ stick) butter, melted	60 mL
1 (10 ounce) can cream of celery soup	1 (284 g)
1 (10 ounce) can fiesta nacho cheese soup	1 (284 g)

- Place potatoes, green beans and minced onions in slow cooker sprayed with vegetable cooking spray.

- Pour melted butter over vegetables.

- In saucepan, combine both soups and ⅓ cup (80 mL) water. Heat just enough to be able to mix soups and pour over vegetables.

- Cover and cook on LOW for 7 to 8 hours.

Green Beans to Enjoy

About 2 pounds fresh green beans	1 kg
1 onion, finely chopped	1
4 thick slices bacon	4
5 to 6 medium new potatoes	5 to 6
1½ teaspoons salt	7 mL
1 teaspoon sugar	5 mL

- Snap and wash green beans, place beans and onion in slow cooker.

- Cut bacon in 1-inch pieces and fry in skillet until crisp.

- Remove some of deeper "eyes" in new potatoes and cut into quarters.

- Spray sides of 5 to 6-quart (5 to 6 L) slow cooker with vegetable cooking spray.

- Add cooked bacon pieces, potatoes and 1 cup (250 mL) water.

- Add about 1½ teaspoons salt (7 mL) and scant teaspoon (5 mL) sugar. (A touch of sugar always helps fresh vegetables.)

- Cover and cook on LOW for 3 to 4 hours.

Green Bean Revenge

2 (16 ounce) packages frozen whole green beans, thawed	2 (454 g)
2 (8 ounce) cans sliced water chestnuts, drained	2 (225 g)
1 (16 ounce) package cubed jalapeno processed cheese	1 (450 g)
1 (10 ounce) can tomatoes and green chilies	1 (284 g)
4 tablespoons (½ stick) butter, melted	60 mL
1 tablespoon chicken seasoning	15 mL
1½ cups slightly crushed potato chips	375 mL

- In slow cooker, combine green beans, water chestnuts, cubed cheese, tomatoes, green chilies, melted butter and chicken seasoning and mix well.

- Cover and cook on LOW for 3 to 5 hours.

- (If you would like this to be a one-dish meal, add 2 to 3 cups [500 to 750 mL] cubed, cooked ham.)

- Just before serving, cover top with crushed potato chips.

Crunchy Green Beans

2 (16 ounce) packages frozen whole green beans, thawed	2 (454 mL)
3 ribs celery, diagonally sliced	3
1 sweet red bell pepper, julienned	1
2 (11 ounce) cans sliced water chestnuts, drained	2 (310 g)
1 (10 ounce) can cream of chicken soup	1 (284 g)
½ cup slivered almonds	125 mL
1 (3 ounce) can french-fried onion rings	1 (85 g)

- In slow cooker sprayed with vegetable cooking spray, combine green beans, celery, bell pepper, water chestnuts, chicken soup and almonds.

- Cover and cook on LOW for 2 to 4 hours. About 10 minutes before serving, top with fried onion rings.

A Different Bean

3 (15 ounce) cans black beans, rinsed, drained	3 (438 g)
3 (15 ounce) cans great northern beans, rinsed, drained	3 (438 g)
1 (16 ounce) jar hot, thick and chunky salsa	1 (454 g)
½ cup packed brown sugar	125 mL

- Combine black beans, northern beans, salsa and brown sugar in 5 to 6-quart (6 L) slow cooker.

- Cover and cook on LOW for 3 to 4 hours.

- To include pinto beans in this dish, use only 2 cans black beans and 1 can pinto beans.

Beans and More Beans

4 slices thick sliced bacon, cooked crisp, crumbled	4
1 (15 ounce) can kidney beans, drained	1 (438 g)
1 (15 ounce) can lima beans, liquid reserved	1 (438 g)
1 (15 ounce) can pinto beans, liquid reserved	1 (438 g)
1 (15 ounce) can navy beans, liquid reserved	1 (438 g)
1 (15 ounce) can pork and beans, liquid reserved	1 (438 g)
1 onion, chopped	1
¾ cup chili sauce	175 mL
1 cup packed brown sugar	250 mL
1 tablespoon worcestershire sauce	15 mL

- In sprayed slow cooker, combine all ingredients and mix well.

- Cover and cook on LOW for 5 to 6 hours.

Better Butter Beans

2 cups sliced celery	500 mL
2 onions, chopped	2
1 green bell pepper, julienned	1
1 (15 ounce) can stewed tomatoes	1 (438 g)
4 tablespoons (½ stick) butter, melted	60 mL
1 tablespoon chicken seasoning	15 mL
3 (15 ounce) cans butter beans, drained	3 (438 g)

- In slow cooker, combine all ingredients and mix well.

- (If you would like this to be a one-dish dinner, add 2 to 3 cups [500 to 750 mL] cubed, cooked ham.)

- Cover and cook on LOW for 3 to 4 hours.

Italian Beans

2 (15 ounce) cans garbanzo beans, drained	2 (438 g)
1 (15 ounce) can red kidney beans, drained	1 (438 g)
1 (15 ounce) can cannelloni (white kidney beans), drained	1 (438 g)
2 (15 ounce) cans great northern beans, drained	2 (438 g)
1 teaspoon Italian seasoning	5 mL
1 (1 ounce) envelope dry onion soup mix	1 (28 g)
1 teaspoon prepared minced garlic	5 mL
½ cup beef broth	125 mL

- Combine all ingredients in slow cooker and stir well.

- Cover and cook on LOW for 5 to 6 hours or on HIGH for 2½ to 3 hours.

Creamy Limas

2 (16 ounce) packages frozen baby lima beans, thawed	2 (454 g)
1 (10 ounce) can cream of celery	1 (284 g)
1 (10 ounce) can cream of onion soup	1 (284 g)
1 sweet red bell pepper, julienned	1
1 (4 ounce) jar sliced mushrooms, drained	1 (113 g)
¼ cup milk	50 mL
1 cup shredded cheddar-colby cheese	250 mL

- In 4 or 6-quart (6 L) slow cooker, combine lima beans, both soups, bell pepper, mushrooms and ½ teaspoon (2 mL) salt and stir well.

- Cover and cook on LOW for 8 to 9 hours.

- Just before serving, stir in milk, remove limas to serving bowl and sprinkle cheese over top.

Chili Frijoles

2 cups dry pinto beans	500 mL
2 onions, finely chopped	2
2 tablespoons chili powder	30 mL
1 teaspoon prepared minced garlic	5 mL
1 (15 ounce) can tomato sauce	1 (438 g)
1½ pounds lean ground beef	750 g
1 tablespoon salt	15 mL

- Place beans in large saucepan and cover with water. Bring to boiling, turn off heat and let stand 1 hour.

- Drain and transfer beans to large slow cooker. Add onion, chili powder, garlic, tomato sauce, salt and 8 cups (2 L) water.

- In skillet, brown ground beef, drain and transfer to cooker.

- Cover, cook on LOW for 8 to 9 hours or until beans are tender and stir occasionally.

Cajun Beans and Rice

1 pound dry black beans	500 g
2 onions, chopped	2
2 teaspoons minced garlic	10 mL
1 tablespoon ground cumin	15 mL
2 teaspoons salt	10 mL
1 (14 ounce) can chicken broth	1 (420 g)
1 cup instant brown rice	250 mL

- Place beans in saucepan, cover with water and soak overnight.

- In 4 or 5-quart (5 L) slow cooker, combine beans, onion, garlic, cumin, salt, chicken broth and 2 cups (500 mL) water.

- Cover and cook on LOW for 4 to 6 hours.

- Stir in instant rice, cover and cook another 20 minutes.

TIP: If soaking beans overnight is not an option, place beans in saucepan and add enough water to cover by 2 inches. Bring to boil, reduce heat and simmer for 10 minutes. Let stand 1 hour, drain and rinse beans.

Cinnamon Carrots

2 (16 ounce) packages baby carrots	2 (454 g)
¾ cup packed brown sugar	175 mL
¼ cup honey	60 mL
½ cup orange juice	125 mL
2½ tablespoons (⅓ stick) butter, melted	37 mL
¾ teaspoon ground cinnamon	4 mL

- Place carrots in 3 to 4-quart (4 L) slow cooker sprayed with vegetable cooking spray.

- In bowl, combine brown sugar, honey, orange juice, butter and cinnamon and mix well.

- Pour over carrots and mix so sugar-cinnamon mixture coats carrots.

- Cover and cook on LOW for 3½ to 4 hours and stir twice during cooking time.

- About 20 minutes before serving, transfer carrots with a slotted spoon to serving dish and cover to keep warm.

- Pour liquid from cooker into a saucepan; boil for several minutes until liquid is reduced by half. Spoon over carrots in serving dish.

Krazy Karrots

1 (16 ounce) package baby carrots	1 (454 g)
4 tablespoons (½ stick) butter, melted	60 mL
⅔ cup packed brown sugar	150 mL
1 (1 ounce) packet ranch dressing mix	1 (28g)

- In 4-quart (4 L) slow cooker, combine carrots, melted butter, brown sugar, ranch dressing mix and ¼ cup (60 mL) water and stir well.

- Cover and cook on low for 3 to 4 hours and stir occasionally.

Squash Combo

1½ pounds small yellow squash	750 g
1½ pounds zucchini	750 g
1 teaspoon seasoned salt	5 mL
¼ cup (½ stick) butter, melted	60 mL
½ cup seasoned dry breadcrumbs	125 mL
½ cup grated cheddar cheese	125 mL

- Cut both yellow squash and zucchini in small pieces.

- Place in bottom of slow cooker sprayed with vegetable cooking spray.

- Sprinkle with seasoned salt and pepper.

- Pour melted butter over squash and sprinkle with breadcrumbs and cheese.

- Cover and cook on LOW for 5 to 6 hours.

Sunny Yellow Squash

2 pounds small-medium yellow squash, sliced	1 kg
2 onions, coarsely chopped	2
3 ribs celery, diagonally sliced	3
1 green bell pepper, julienned	1
1 (8 ounce) package cream cheese, cubed	1 (227 g)
1 teaspoon sugar	5 mL
1 teaspoon white pepper	5 mL
¼ cup (½ stick) butter, melted	60 mL
1 (10 ounce) can cheddar cheese soup	1 (284 g)
1½ cups seasoned croutons	375 mL
1 teaspoon salt	5 mL

- In slow cooker, combine all ingredients, except croutons and 1 teaspoon (5 mL) salt and mix well.

- Cover and cook on LOW for 3 to 4 hours.

- Before serving, sprinkle top with croutons.

Golden Squash

1 pound yellow squash, thinly sliced	500g
1 pound zucchini, thinly sliced	500g
3 ribs celery, sliced	3
1 onion, chopped	1
1 (10 ounce) can cream of chicken soup	1 (284 g)
1 (8 ounce) carton sour cream	1 (227 g)
3 tablespoons flour	45 mL
1 (6 ounce) package seasoned stuffing mix	1 (170 g)
½ cup (1 stick) butter, melted	125 mL

- In large bowl, combine squash, zucchini, celery, onion and soup.

- Mix sour cream with flour and stir into vegetables. Toss stuffing with melted butter and spoon half into slow cooker.

- Top with vegetables and spoon remaining stuffing on top.

- Cover and cook on LOW for 5 to 7 hours.

Super Corn

2 (15 ounce) cans whole kernel corn	2 (438 g)
2 (15 ounce) cans creamed corn	2 (438 g)
½ cup (1 stick) butter, melted	125 mL
1 (8 ounce) carton sour cream	1 (227 g)
1 (8 ounce) package jalapeno cornbread mix	1 (227 g)

- In large bowl, combine all ingredients and mix well.

- Pour into slow cooker sprayed with vegetable cooking spray.

- Cover and cook on LOW for 4 to 5 hours.

- Make this a one-dish meal by adding 2 to 3 cups (500 to 750 mL) cubed, leftover ham.

Yummy Corn

1 (8 ounce) package cream cheese	1 (227 g)
1 (3 ounce) package cream cheese	1 (85 g)
½ cup (1 stick) butter, melted	125 mL
2 (16 ounce) packages frozen whole kernel corn, thawed	2 (454 g)
½ teaspoon white pepper	2 mL

- In 4-quart (4 L) slow cooker prepared with vegetable cooking spray, turn cooker heat to HIGH and add cream cheese and butter.

- Cook just until cheese and butter melt and stir. Add corn, white pepper and a little salt.

- Cover and cook on LOW for 1½ to 2 hours.

Creamed Peas and Potatoes

2 pounds small new potatoes, unpeeled, quartered	1 kg
1 (16 ounce) package frozen green peas with pearl onions, thawed	1 (454 g)
2 (10 ounce) cans fiesta nacho cheese soup	2 (284 g)
½ cup milk	125 mL

- Sprinkle potatoes with salt and pepper, place in slow cooker sprayed with vegetable cooking spray and place peas on top.

- In saucepan, combine nacho cheese soup and milk, heat just enough to mix well and spoon over peas.

- Cover and cook on LOW for 4 to 5 hours.

Creamed-Cheese Spinach

2 (10 ounce) packages frozen chopped spinach, thawed, well drained	1 (284 g)
1 (16 ounce) carton small-curd cottage cheese	1 (454 g)
1½ cups shredded American or cheddar cheese	375 mL
3 eggs, beaten	3
¼ cup (½ stick) butter, melted	60 mL
¼ cup flour	60 mL

- Drain spinach with paper towels and drain again with new paper towels to press out all liquid.

- In mixing bowl, combine all ingredients and mix well.

- Spoon into slow cooker sprayed with vegetable cooking spray.

- Cover and cook on HIGH for 1 hour, change heat to LOW and cook another 3 to 5 hours or until knife inserted in center comes out clean.

Cheese-Please Spinach

1 (10 ounce) package chopped spinach, thawed, drained	1 (284 g)
1 (16 ounce) package chopped spinach, thawed, drained	1 (454 g)
1 (8 ounce) package cream cheese, cubed, softened	1 (227 g)
1 (10 ounce) can cream of chicken soup	1 (284 g)
1 egg, beaten	1
1 (8 ounce) package shredded cheddar cheese	1 (227 g)

- Drain spinach with paper towels and drain again to press out all liquid.

- In large bowl, combine spinach, cream cheese, chicken soup, egg and salt and pepper to taste. Spoon into slow cooker sprayed with vegetable cooking spray.

- Cover and cook on LOW for 3 to 4 hours.

- Before serving, stir in cheddar cheese.

Healthy Veggies

1 (16 ounce) package frozen broccoli, cauliflower and carrots	1 (454 g)
2 medium zucchini, halved lengthwise, sliced	2
1 (1.3 ounce) packet ranch dressing mix	1 (32 g)
2 tablespoons (¼ stick) butter, melted	30 mL

- Place broccoli, cauliflower, carrots and zucchini in 4-quart (4L) slow cooker.

- Combine ranch dressing mix, melted butter and ½ cup (125 mL) water, spoon over vegetables and stir.

- Cover and cook on LOW for 2 to 3 hours.

Harvest-Vegetable Casserole

3 or 4 medium new potatoes, unpeeled, sliced	3 to 4
2 onions, sliced	2
3 carrots, sliced	3
2 cups chopped green cabbage	500 mL
¼ cup Italian dressing	60 mL
1 (1 pound) ring kielbasa sausage	1 (500 g)
1 (15 ounce) can Italian stewed tomatoes	1 (438 g)

- In large slow cooker, place potatoes, onions, carrots and cabbage.

- Cut sausage into 1-inch pieces and place on top of vegetables.

- Drizzle stewed tomatoes in even layers over vegetables.

- Cover and cook on LOW for 6 to 8 hours or until vegetables are tender.

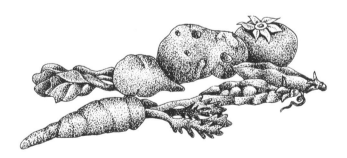

California Vegetables

1 (16 ounce) package frozen vegetables (broccoli, cauliflower, carrots), thawed	1 (454 g)
1 (10 ounce) package frozen green peas, thawed	1 (284 g)
1 (10 ounce) package frozen whole kernel corn, thawed	1 (284 g)
2 (10 ounce) cans cream of mushroom soup	2 (284 g)
1 cup instant white rice	250 mL
1 (8 ounce) package cubed processed cheese	1 (227 g)
1 cup milk	250 mL
2 tablespoons (¼ stick) butter, melted	30 mL
1 teaspoon seasoned salt	5 mL

- Place all vegetables in large slow cooker sprayed with vegetable cooking spray.

- In bowl, combine soup, rice, cubed cheese, milk, butter, seasoned salt and 1 cup (250 mL) water and pour over vegetables.

- Cover and cook on LOW for 4 to 5 hours. Stir before serving.

Golden Veggies

1 (16 ounce) package frozen cauliflower florets, thawed	1 (454 g)
1 (15 ounce) can whole kernel corn	1 (438 g)
¾ pound small yellow squash, chopped	340 g
¼ cup (½ stick) butter, melted	60 mL
2 (10 ounce) cans cheddar cheese soup	2 (284 g)
6 slices bacon, cooked, crumbled	6

- Place cauliflower, corn and squash in slow cooker and sprinkle with salt and pepper.

- Pour melted butter over vegetables and spoon cheese soups on top. Sprinkle with crumbled bacon.

- Cover and cook on LOW for 4 to 5 hours.

Four-Veggie Bake

1 (10 ounce) package frozen broccoli florets, thawed	1 (284 g)
1 (10 ounce) package frozen cauliflower, thawed	1 (284 g)
1 (10 ounce) package frozen brussels sprouts	1 (284 g)
4 small yellow squash, sliced	4
1 (10 ounce) can cream of mushroom soup	1 (284 g)
1 (16 ounce) package cubed processed cheese	1 (454 g)

- Place vegetables in slow cooker sprayed with vegetable cooking spray.

- Layer soup and cheese on top of vegetables.

- Cover and cook on LOW for 3 to 4 hours.

Potatoes al Grande

6 medium potatoes, peeled	6
1 (8 ounce) package shredded cheddar cheese, divided	1 (227 g)
1 (10 ounce) can cream of chicken soup	1 (284 g)
¼ cup (½ stick) butter, melted	60 mL
1 (8 ounce) carton sour cream	1 (227 g)
1 (3 ounce) can french-fried onion rings	1 (85 g)

- Cut potatoes in 1-inch strips. Toss potatoes with some salt and pepper plus 2 cups (500 mL) cheese. Place in slow cooker.

- Combine soup, melted butter and 2 tablespoons (30 mL) water and pour over potato mixture.

- Cover and cook on low for 6 to 8 hours or until potatoes are tender.

- Stir in sour cream and remaining cheese.

- When ready to serve, sprinkle onion rings over top of potatoes.

Pretty Parsley Potatoes

2 pounds small new potatoes, unpeeled, quartered	**1 kg**
¼ cup vegetable oil	**60 mL**
1 (1.3 ounce) packet ranch dressing mix	**1 (32 g)**
¼ cup fresh chopped parsley	**60 mL**

- Place potatoes, vegetable oil, dressing mix and ¼ cup (60 mL) water in 4 to 5-quart (5 L) slow cooker and toss to coat potatoes.

- Cover and cook on LOW for 3 to 4 hours or until potatoes are tender.

- When ready to serve, sprinkle parsley over potatoes and toss.

Roasted New Potatoes

18 to 20 new potatoes, unpeeled	**18 to 20**
¼ cup (½ stick) butter, melted	**60 mL**
1 tablespoon dried parsley	**15 mL**
½ teaspoon garlic powder	**2 mL**
½ teaspoon salt	**2 mL**
½ teaspoon black pepper	**2 mL**
½ teaspoon paprika	**2 mL**

- Combine all ingredients into slow cooker and mix well.

- Cover and cook on LOW for 7 hours or on HIGH for 3½ to 4 hours.

- When ready to serve, remove potatoes with slotted spoon to serving dish and cover to keep warm.

- Add about 2 tablespoons (30 mL) water to drippings and stir until well blended.

- Pour mixture over potatoes.

Good Old Cheesy Potatoes

1 (28 ounce) package frozen hash brown potatoes with onions and peppers, thawed	1 (800 g)
2 (10 ounce) cans cream of chicken soup	2 (284 g)
1 (8 ounce) carton sour cream	1 (227 g)
½ cup (1 stick) butter, melted, divided	125 mL
1 (8 ounce) package grated cheddar cheese	1 (227 g)
2 tablespoons dried parsley	30 mL
2 cups dry stuffing mix	500 mL

- Place hash brown in large bowl, add soups, sour cream, ¼ cup (½ stick) melted butter, cheese, parsley and about 1 teaspoon (5 mL) salt and mix well.

- Spoon into large slow cooker. Sprinkle stuffing mix over potato mixture and drizzle remaining butter over stuffing.

- Cover and cook on LOW for 7 to 9 hours or on HIGH for 3 to 4 hours.

Glory Potatoes

1 (10 ounce) can cream of chicken soup	1 (284 g)
1 (8 ounce) carton sour cream	1 (227 g)
2 pounds potatoes, peeled, cubed	1 kg
1 (8 ounce) package shredded cheddar-jack cheese	1 (227 g)
1 cup crushed potato chips	250 mL

- In bowl combine soup, sour cream, some salt and pepper and ¼ cup (50 mL) water.

- Combine potatoes and cheese in 5-quart (5 L) slow cooker. Spoon soup-sour cream mixture over potatoes.

- Cover and cook on LOW for 8 to 9 hours.

- When ready to serve, sprinkle crushed potato chips over potatoes.

Easy Baked Potatoes

10 medium unpeeled russet potatoes	**10**
¼ to ½ cup oil	**60 mL to**
	125 mL

Salt and pepper
Butter
Sour cream

- Pierce potatoes with fork. Brush potato skins with oil and sprinkle salt and pepper on potato skins.

- Wrap potatoes individually in foil and place in large slow cooker.

- Cover and cook on LOW for 7 to 8 hours or until potatoes are tender.

- Prepare assorted toppings such as: shredded cheese, salsa, ranch dip, chopped green onions, bacon bits, chopped boiled eggs, cheese-hamburger dip, broccoli-cheese soup, etc.

Dressed-Up Hash Browns

1 (26 ounce) package frozen hash brown with onion and peppers, thawed	1 (775 g)
2 to 3 cups cooked, chopped ham	500 g to 750 mL
1 (16 ounce) carton sour cream	1 (454 g)
1 (8 ounce) package shredded cheddar-jack cheese	1 (227 g)
1 (3 ounce) can french-fried onion rings	1 (85 g)

- In large skillet, brown hash browns in a little oil. Transfer to 5 to 6-quart (6 L) slow cooker.

- Combine ham, sour cream and cheese and mix into hash browns.

- Cover and cook on LOW for 2 to 3 hours.

- Dress these potatoes up by sprinkling onion rings on top of cheese.

Creamed New Potatoes

2 to 2½ pounds new potatoes, unpeeled, quartered	1 to 1.25 kg
1 (8 ounce) package cream cheese, softened	1 (227 g)
1 (10 ounce) can fiesta nacho soup	1 (284 g)
1 (1 ounce) envelope buttermilk ranch salad dressing mix	1 (28 g)
1 cup milk	250 mL

- Place potatoes in 6-quart (6 L) slow cooker.

- With mixer, beat cream cheese until creamy and fold in fiesta nacho soup, ranch salad dressing mix and milk. Stir into potatoes.

- Cover and cook on LOW for 3 to 4 hours or until potatoes are well done.

Company Potatoes

1 (4.9 ounce) box scalloped potatoes	1 (140 g)
1 (4.9 ounce) box au gratin potatoes	1 (140 g)
1 cup milk	250 mL
6 tablespoons (¾ stick) butter, melted	90 mL
½ pound bacon, cooked crisp, crumbled	250 g

- Place both boxes of potatoes in slow cooker sprayed with vegetable cooking spray.

- In bowl combine milk, butter and 4¼ cups (1.25 L) water and pour over potatoes.

- Cover and cook on LOW for 4 to 5 hours.

- When ready to serve, sprinkle crumbled bacon over top of potatoes.

Cheezy Potatoes

1 (28 ounce) bag frozen diced potatoes with onions and peppers, thawed	1 (800 g)
1 (8 ounce) package shredded Monterey Jack and cheddar cheese blend	1 (227 g)
1 (10 ounce) can cream of celery soup	1 (284 g)
1 (8 ounce) carton sour cream	1 (227 g)
1 teaspoon white pepper	5 mL

- In sprayed 5 or 6-quart (6 L) slow cooker, combine potatoes, cheese, soup, sour cream and pepper and mix well.

- Cover and cook on LOW 4 to 6 hours. Stir well before serving.

Cheesy Ranch Potatoes

2½ pounds new potatoes, unpeeled, quartered	1.25 kg
1 onion, cut into 8 parts	1
1 (10 ounce) can fiesta nacho cheese soup	1 (284 g)
1 (8 ounce) carton sour cream	1 (227 g)
1 (1 ounce) package dry ranch salad dressing mix	1 (28 g)
Chopped fresh parsley, optional	

- Place potatoes and onion in 4 to 5-quart (5 L) slow cooker.

- In bowl, combine, nacho cheese, sour cream and dressing mix and stir well to mix.

- Cover and cook on LOW for 6 to 7 hours.

- To serve, sprinkle chopped fresh parsley over potato mixture.

Sweet Potatoes and Pineapple

3 (15 ounce) cans sweet potatoes, drained	3 (438 g)
½ (20 ounce) can pineapple pie filling	570 g
2 tablespoons (¼ stick) butter, melted	30 mL
½ cup brown sugar	125 mL
½ teaspoon cinnamon	2 mL

Topping:

1 cup packed light brown sugar	250 mL
3 tablespoons (⅓ stick) butter, melted	45 mL
½ cup flour	125 mL
1 cup coarsely chopped nuts	250 mL

- In 4 to 5-quart (5 L) slow cooker sprayed with vegetable cooking spray.

- Place sweet potatoes, pie filling, melted butter, brown sugar and cinnamon in slow cooker and lightly stir.

- Cover and cook on LOW for 2 to 3 hours.

- While potatoes are cooking, combine topping ingredients, spread on foil-lined cookie sheet and bake at 350° (121° C) for 15 to 20 minutes.

- When ready to serve, sprinkle topping over sweet potatoes.

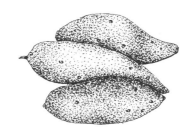

Glazed Sweet Potatoes

3 (15 ounce) cans sweet potatoes, drained	2 (438 g)
¼ cup (½ stick) butter, melted	60 mL
2 cups packed brown sugar	500 mL
⅓ cup orange juice	75 mL
⅛ teaspoon salt	.5 mL
½ teaspoon ground cinnamon	2 mL

- After draining sweet potatoes, cut into smaller chunks and place them in 4 to 5-quart (5 L) slow cooker.

- Add butter, brown sugar, orange juice, salt and a little sprinkle of cinnamon and stir well.

- Cover and cook on LOW for 4 to 5 hours.

Hoppin' John

3 (15 ounce) cans black-eyed peas, liquid reserved	3 (438 g)
1 onion, chopped	1
1 (6.2 ounce) package parmesan and butter rice	1 (180 g)
2 cups cooked, chopped ham	500 mL
2 tablespoons (¼ stick) butter, melted	30 mL

- In slow cooker, combine peas, onion, rice mix, ham, butter and 1¾ cups (425 mL) water and mix well.

- Cover and cook on LOW for 2 to 4 hours.

Spicy Spanish Rice

1½ cups uncooked white rice	375 mL
1 (10 ounce) can diced tomatoes and green chilies	1 (284 g)
1 (15 ounce) can stewed tomatoes	1 (438 g)
1 (1 ounce) envelope taco seasoning	1 (28 g)
1 large onion, chopped	1

- In 5-quart (5 L) slow cooker, combine all ingredients plus 2 cups (500 mL) water and stir well.

- Cover and cook on LOW for 5 to 7 hours. The flavor will go through the rice better if you stir 2 or 3 times during cooking time.

- Make this "a main dish" by adding 1 pound (500 g) Polish sausage slices to rice mixture.

Delicious Risotto Rice

1½ cups risotto Italian-style rice	375 mL
3 (14 ounce) cans chicken broth	1 (420 g)
3 tablespoons (⅓ stick) butter, melted	45 mL
1½ cups fresh mushrooms, sliced	375 mL
1 cup sliced celery	250 mL

- In 4 to 5-quart (5 L) slow cooker, combine rice, chicken broth, butter, mushrooms and celery.

- Cover and cook on LOW for 2 to 3 hours or until rice is tender.

Crunchy Couscous

When rice seems boring, try couscous.

1 (10 ounce) box original plain couscous	1 (284 g)
2 cups sliced celery	500 mL
1 sweet red bell pepper, chopped	1
1 yellow bell pepper, chopped	1
1 (16 ounce) jar creamy alfredo sauce	1 (454 g)

- In 5-quart (5 L) slow cooker, combine couscous, celery, chopped bell peppers, alfredo sauce and 1½ cups (375 mL) water and mix well.

- Cover and cook on LOW for 2 hours, stir once or twice.

- Check slow cooker to make sure celery and peppers are cooked, but still crunchy.

Carnival Couscous

1 (5.7 ounce) box herbed-chicken couscous	1 (180 g)
1 red bell pepper, julienned	1
1 green bell pepper, julienned	1
2 small yellow squash, sliced	2
1 (16 ounce) package frozen mixed vegetables, thawed	1 (454 g)
1 (10 ounce) can French onion soup	1 (284 g)
¼ cup (½ stick) butter, melted	60 mL
½ teaspoon seasoned salt	2 mL

- In slow cooker sprayed with vegetable cooking spray, combine all ingredients plus 1½ cups (375 mL) water and mix well.

- Cover and cook on LOW for 2 to 4 hours.

Cheese-Spaghetti and Spinach

1 (7 ounce) box ready-cut spaghetti	1 (198 g)
2 tablespoons butter	30 mL
1(8 ounce) carton sour cream	1 (227 g)
1 cup shredded cheddar cheese	250 mL
1 (8 ounce) package Monterey Jack cheese, divided	1 (227 g)
1 (12 ounce) package frozen, chopped spinach, thawed, very well drained	1 (340 g)
1 (6 ounce) can cheddar french-fried onions, divided	1 (170 g)

- Cook spaghetti according to package directions, drain and stir in butter until it melts.

- Grease sides and bottom of slow cooker. In large bowl, combine sour cream, cheddar cheese, half Monterey Jack cheese, spinach and half can onions. Fold into spaghetti and spoon into slow cooker.

- Cover and cook on LOW for 2 to 4 hours.

- When ready to serve, sprinkle remaining Jack cheese and fried onion rings over top.

St. Pat's Noodles

1 (12 ounce) package uncooked medium noodles	1 (340 g)
1 cup half-and-half cream	250 mL
1 (10 ounce) package frozen chopped spinach, thawed	1 (284 g)
6 tablespoons (¾ stick) butter, melted	90 mL
2 teaspoons seasoned salt	10 mL
1½ cups shredded cheddar-jack cheese	375 mL

- In saucepan, cook noodles according to package directions and drain.

- Place in 5 to 6-quart (6 L) slow cooker.   Add half-and-half, spinach, butter and seasoned salt and stir until well blended.

- Cover and cook on LOW for 2 to 3 hours.

- When ready to serve, fold in cheese.

CHICKEN

Chicken Olé

6 boneless, skinless chicken breast halves	6
1 (8 ounce) package cream cheese, softened	1 (227g)
1 (16 ounce) jar salsa	1 (454g)
2 teaspoons cumin	10 mL
1 bunch fresh green onions with tops, chopped	1

- Pound chicken breasts to flatten. In mixing bowl, beat cream cheese until smooth and add salsa, cumin and onions.

- Place heaping spoonfuls of cream cheese mixture on each chicken breast and roll up. (There will be leftover cream cheese mixture.)

- Place chicken breast seam side-down in slow cooker sprayed with vegetable cooking spray. Spoon remaining cream cheese mixture over each chicken roll.

- Cover and cook on LOW for 5 to 6 hours.

Chicken for the Gods

1¾ cups flour	425 mL
Scant 2 tablespoons dry mustard	30 mL
6 boneless, skinless chicken breast halves	6
2 tablespoons oil	30 mL
1 (10 ounce) can condensed chicken and rice soup	1 (284g)

- Place flour and mustard in shallow bowl and dredge chicken breasts.

- In skillet, brown chicken breasts in oil. Place all breasts in oblong 6-quart (6 L) slow cooker.

- Pour chicken and rice soup over chicken and add about ¼ (60 mL) cup water.

- Cover and cook on LOW for 6 to 7 hours.

Apricot Chicken

6 boneless, skinless chicken breasts halves	6
1 (12 ounce) jar apricot preserves	1 (340g)
1 (8 ounce) bottle Catalina dressing	1 (228g)
1 (1 ounce) package dry onion soup mix	1 (28 g)

- Place chicken in 6-quart (6 L) slow cooker sprayed with vegetable cooking spray.

- Combine apricot preserves, Catalina dressing, onion soup mix and ¼ cup (60 mL) water and stir well. Cover chicken breasts with sauce mixture.

- Cover and cook on LOW for 5 to 6 hours.

Artichoke-Chicken Pasta

1½ pounds boneless chicken breast tenders	750 g
1 (15 ounce) can artichoke hearts, quartered	1 (438 g)
¾ cup roasted red peppers, chopped	175 mL
1 (8 ounce) package American cheese, shredded	1 (227 g)
1 tablespoon white wine worcestershire sauce	15 mL
1 (10 ounce) can cream of chicken soup	1 (284 g)
1 (8 ounce) package shredded cheddar cheese	1 (227 g)
4 cups hot, cooked bow-tie pasta	1 L

- In slow cooker, combine chicken tenders, artichoke, roasted peppers, American cheese, worcestershire sauce and soup and mix well.

- Cover and cook on LOW for 6 to 8 hours.

- About 20 minutes before serving, fold in cheddar cheese, hot pasta, salt and pepper to taste.

Broccoli-Rice Chicken

1¼ cups uncooked converted rice	30 mL
2 pounds boneless, skinless chicken breast halves	1 kg
Dried parsley	
Black pepper	
1 (1.8 ounce) package cream of broccoli soup mix	1 (50 g)
1 (14 ounce) can chicken broth	1 (420 g)

- Place rice in lightly greased slow cooker. Cut chicken into slices and put over rice.

- Sprinkle with parsley and black pepper.

- In saucepan, combine soup mix and chicken broth and 1 cup (250 mL) water. Heat just enough to mix well. Pour over chicken and rice.

- Cover and cook on LOW for 6 to 8 hours.

Bacon-Wrapped Chicken

1 (2.5 ounce) jar dried beef	1 (71 g)
6 boneless, skinless chicken breast halves	6
6 slices bacon	6
2 (10 ounce) cans golden mushroom soup	2 (284 g)
1 (6.2 ounce) package parmesan and butter rice, cooked	1 (170 g)

- Place slices of dried beef in bottom of 5-quart (5 L) slow cooker.

- Roll each chicken breast half in slice of bacon. Place over dried beef.

- Spoon mushroom soup and ⅓ (75 mL) cup water over chicken.

- Cover and cook on LOW for 7 to 8 hours. Serve over hot cooked rice.

Broccoli-Cheese Chicken

4 boned, skinless chicken breast halves	4
2 tablespoons (¼ stick) butter, melted	30 mL
1 (10 ounce) can broccoli cheese soup	1 (284 g)
¼ cup milk	60 mL
1 (10 ounce) package frozen broccoli spears	1 (284 g)

- Dry chicken breasts with paper towels and place in oblong slow cooker sprayed with vegetable cooking spray.

- In bowl, combine melted butter, soup and milk and spoon over chicken.

- Cover and cook on LOW for 4 to 6 hours.

- Remove cooker lid and place broccoli over chicken. Cover and cook 1 more hour. Serve over hot buttered rice.

Cream Cheese Chicken

4 boneless, skinless chicken breast halves	4
2 tablespoons (¼ stick) butter, melted	30 mL
1 (10 ounce) can cream of mushroom soup	1 (284 g)
2 tablespoons dried Italian salad dressing	30 mL
½ cup sherry	125 mL
1 (8 ounce) package cream cheese, cubed	1 (227 g)

- Wash chicken breast, dry with paper towels and brush melted butter over chicken.

- Place in oblong slow cooker and add remaining ingredients.

- Cover and cook on LOW for 6 to 7 hours. Serve over hot buttered noodles.

Chicken and Noodles

2 pounds boneless, skinless chicken breast halves	**1 kg**
¼ cup cornstarch	**60 mL**
⅓ cup soy sauce	**75 mL**
2 onions, chopped	**2**
3 ribs celery, sliced diagonally	**3**
1 sweet red bell pepper, julienned	**1**
2 (14 ounce) cans mixed Chinese vegetables, drained	**1 (420 g)**
¼ cup molasses	**60 mL**

- Place chicken breasts and 2 cups (500 mL) water in slow cooker, cover and cook on LOW for 3 to 4 hours.

- One hour before serving, remove chicken and cut into bite-size pieces.

- In bowl, combine cornstarch and soy sauce and mix well. Stir into slow cooker.

- Add onions, celery, bell pepper, mixed vegetables and molasses. Turn heat to HIGH and cook for 1 to 2 hours.

- Serve over chow mein noodles.

Chicken and Pasta

1 (16 ounce) package frozen whole green beans, thawed	1 (454 g)
1 onion, chopped	1
1 cup fresh mushrooms, halved	250 mL
3 boneless, skinless chicken breast halves, cut in 1-inch pieces	3
1 (15 ounce) can Italian stewed tomatoes	1 (438 g)
1 teaspoon chicken bouillon	5 mL
1 teaspoon minced garlic	5 mL
1 teaspoon Italian seasoning	5 mL
1 (8 ounce) package fettuccine	1 (227 g)
1 (4 ounce) package parmesan cheese	1 (113 g)

- Spray 4 to 5-quart (5 L) slow cooker with vegetable cooking spray. Place green beans, onion and mushrooms in bottom of cooker.

- Cut chicken into 1-inch pieces and place over vegetables.

- In small bowl, combine stewed tomatoes, chicken bouillon, garlic and Italian seasoning. Pour over chicken.

- Cover and cook on LOW for 5 to 6 hours.

- Cook fettuccine according to package directions and drain.

- Serve chicken over fettuccine sprinkled with parmesan cheese.

- Add ¼ cup (½ stick) (60 mL) butter to make this dish even better.

Chicken and Vegetables

4 to 5 boneless, skinless chicken breast halves	4 to 5
2 teaspoons seasoned salt	10 mL
1 (16 ounce) package frozen broccoli, cauliflower and carrots, thawed	1 (454 g)
1 (10 ounce) can cream of celery soup	1 (284 g)
1 (8 ounce) package shredded cheddar- jack cheese	1 (227 g)

- Cut chicken into strips and place chicken strips sprinkled with seasoned salt in slow cooker sprayed with vegetable cooking spray.

- In large bowl, combine vegetables, celery soup and half cheese and mix well. Spoon over chicken breasts.

- Cover and cook on LOW for 4 to 5 hours.

- About 10 minutes before serving, sprinkle remaining cheese on top of casserole.

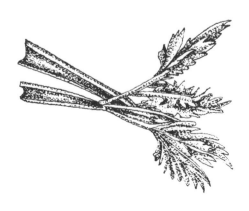

Chicken Curry Over Rice

3 boneless, skinless chicken breast halves, cut into thin strips	3
½ cup chicken broth	125 mL
1 (10 ounce) can cream of chicken soup	1 (284 g)
1 onion, coarsely chopped	1
1 sweet red bell pepper, julienned	1
¼ cup golden raisins	60 mL
1½ teaspoons curry powder	7 mL
¼ teaspoon ground ginger	1 mL

- Cut chicken into thin strips.

- In 5 to 6-quart (6 L) slow cooker sprayed with vegetable cooking spray, combine chicken strips, broth, soup, onion, bell pepper, raisins, curry powder and ginger and mix well.

- Cover and cook on LOW for 3 to 4 hours. Serve over hot cooked rice.

Chicken Delicious

5 to 6 boneless skinless chicken breast halves	5 to 6
1 (16 ounce) package frozen broccoli florets, thawed	1 (454 g)
1 sweet red bell pepper, julienned	1
1 (16 ounce) jar parmesan and mozzarella cheese creation sauce	1 (454 g)
3 tablespoons sherry	45 mL

- In skillet, brown chicken breasts and place in oval 5 to 6-quart (6 L) slow cooker sprayed with vegetable cooking spray.

- Place broccoli florets on plate, remove much of stem and discard.

- In bowl combine broccoli florets, julienne bell pepper, cheese sauce and sherry and mix well. Spoon over chicken breasts.

- Cover and cook on LOW for 4 to 5 hours. Serve over hot buttered noodles.

Chicken Delight

¾ cup white uncooked rice	175 mL
1 (14 ounce) can chicken broth	1 (422 g)
1 (1 ounce) envelope onion soup mix	1 (28 g)
1 sweet red bell pepper, seeded, chopped	1
2 (10 ounce) cans cream of celery soup	2 (284 g)
¾ cup white cooking wine	175 mL
4 to 6 boneless skinless chicken breasts halves	4 to 6
1 (3 ounce) packages fresh parmesan cheese	1 (110 g)

- In bowl, combine rice, broth, soup mix, bell pepper, celery soup, ¾ cup (175 mL) water, wine and several sprinkles of black pepper and mix well. Make sure soup is mixed well with liquids.

- Spray 6-quart (6 L) oval slow cooker with vegetable cooking spray and place chicken breasts in cooker.

- Pour rice-soup mixture over chicken breasts.

- Cover and cook on LOW for 4 to 6 hours.

- 1 hour before serving, sprinkle parmesan cheese over chicken.

Chicken Dinner

1 cup uncooked rice	250 mL
1 tablespoon chicken seasoning	15 mL
1 (1.3 ounce) package dry onion soup mix	1 (32 g)
1 green bell pepper, seeded, chopped	1
1 (4 ounce) jar diced pimentos, drained	1 (113 g)
¾ teaspoon dried basil	4 mL
1 (14 ounce) can chicken broth	1 (420 g)
1 (10 ounce) can cream of chicken soup	1 (284 g)
5 to 6 boneless, skinless chicken breast halves	5 to 6

- In bowl, combine rice, chicken seasoning, onion soup mix, bell pepper, pimentos, basil, broth, ½ cup (125 mL) water and chicken soup and mix well.

- Spoon into oblong slow cooker sprayed with vegetable cooking spray.

- Place chicken breasts in slow cooker and cover chicken with rice mixture.

- Cover and cook on LOW for 6 to 7 hours.

Chicken Fajitas

2 pounds boneless, skinless chicken breast halves	1 kg
1 onion, thinly sliced	1
1 sweet red bell pepper, julienned	1
1 teaspoon ground cumin	5 mL
1½ teaspoons chili powder	7 mL
1 tablespoon lime juice	15 mL
½ cup chicken broth	125 mL
8 to 10 warmed flour tortillas	8 to 10
Guacamole	
Sour cream	
Lettuce and tomatoes	

- Cut chicken into diagonal strips and place in slow cooker sprayed with vegetable cooking spray.

- Top with onion and bell pepper. In bowl, combine cumin, chili powder, lime juice and chicken broth and pour over chicken and vegetables.

- Cover and cook on LOW for 5 to 7 hours.

- When serving, spoon several slices of chicken mixture with sauce into center of each warm tortilla and fold.

- Serve with guacamole, sour cream, lettuce or tomatoes or plain.

Chicken for Supper

5 or 6 boneless, skinless chicken breasts halves	5 or 6
6 carrots, cut in 1-inch lengths	6
1 (15 ounce) can cut green beans, drained	1 (438 g)
1 (15 ounce) can whole new potatoes, drained	1 (438 g)
2 (10 ounce) cans cream of mushroom soup	2 (284 g)
Shredded cheddar cheese	

- Wash, dry chicken breasts with paper towels and place in bottom of oblong slow cooker sprayed with vegetable cooking spray.

- In bowl, combine, carrots, green beans, potatoes and mushroom soup and pour over chicken in cooker.

- Cover and cook on LOW for 8 to 10 hours.

- When ready to serve, sprinkle cheese of top.

Chicken-Ready Supper

1 (6 ounce) package stuffing mix	1 (170 g)
3 cups cooked, chopped chicken breast halves	750 mL
1 (16 ounce) package frozen whole green beans, thawed	1 (450 g)
2 (12 ounce) jars chicken gravy	1 (355 g)

- Prepare stuffing mix according to package directions and place in oblong slow cooker.

- Follow with layer of chopped chicken or leftover turkey breasts and place green beans over chicken. Pour chicken gravy over green beans.

- Cover and cook on LOW for 3½ to 4½ hours.

Chicken Marseilles

4 to 5 boneless, skinless chicken breast halves	4 to 5
2 tablespoons (¼ stick) butter	30 mL
1 (1.8 ounce) package leek soup and dip mix	1 (50 g)
½ teaspoon dillweed	2 mL
1 cup milk	250 mL
¾ cup sour cream	175 mL
Cooked brown rice	

- Place chicken breasts in large slow cooker sprayed with vegetable cooking spray.

- In saucepan, combine butter, leek soup mix, dillweed, milk and ½ cup (125 mL) water and heat just enough for butter to melt and ingredients to mix well. Pour over chicken.

- Cover and cook on LOW for 3 to 5 hours.

- When ready to serve, remove chicken breasts to platter with hot cooked brown rice and cover to keep warm.

- Add sour cream to cooker liquid and stir well. Pour sauce over chicken and rice.

Chicken Breast Deluxe

4 slices bacon	4
5 to 6 boneless, skinless chicken breast halves	5 to 6
1 cup sliced celery	250 mL
1 cup sliced red bell pepper	250 mL
1 (10 ounce) can cream of chicken soup	1 (284g)
2 tablespoons white wine or cooking wine	30 mL
6 slices Swiss cheese	6
2 tablespoons dried parsley	30 mL

- In large skillet, cook bacon, drain, crumble and reserve drippings.

- Place chicken breasts in skillet with bacon drippings and lightly brown on both sides.

- Transfer chicken to oblong slow cooker sprayed with vegetable cooking spray and place celery and red bell pepper over chicken.

- In same skillet, combine soup and wine and spoon over vegetables and chicken.

- Cover and cook on LOW for 3 to 4 hours. Top with slices of cheese over each chicken breast, sprinkle with parsley and cook for an additional 10 minutes.

- Serve with creamy sauce and sprinkle with crumbled bacon.

Chicken Supper

5 boneless, skinless chicken breast halves	5
1 (16 ounce) jar alfredo sauce	1 (454 g)
1 (16 ounce) package frozen green peas, thawed	1 (454 g)
1½ cups shredded mozzarella cheese	375 mL
Hot buttered noodles	

- Cut chicken into strips and place in slow cooker.

- In bowl, combine alfredo sauce, peas and cheese and mix well. Spoon over chicken strips.

- Cover and cook on LOW for 5 to 6 hours.

- When ready to serve, spoon over hot cooked noodles.

Tip: If you want chicken supper in 1 casserole, cook 1 (8 ounce) package noodles and mix with chicken and peas. Sprinkle a little extra cheese over top and serve.

Chicken-Supper Ready

6 medium new potatoes, unpeeled, quartered	6
4 to 5 carrots	4 to 5
4 to 5 boneless, skinless chicken breast halves	4 to 5
1 tablespoon chicken seasoning	15 mL
2 (10 ounce) cans cream of chicken soup	2 (284 g)
1/3 cup white wine or cooking wine	75 mL

- Cut carrots into 1/2-inch pieces. Place potatoes and carrots in slow cooker.

- Sprinkle chicken breasts with chicken seasoning and place over vegetables.

- Spoon soups mixed with 1/4 cup (60 mL) water over chicken and vegetables.

- Cover and cook on LOW for 5 to 6 hours.

TIP: Instead of cream of chicken soup, try 1 (10 ounce) (284 g) can chicken soup and 1 (10 ounce) can mushroom soup for a tasty change.

Chow Mein Chicken

4 boneless, skinless chicken breast halves	4
2 to 3 cups sliced celery	2 to 3
1 onion, coarsely chopped	1
⅓ cup soy sauce	75 mL
¼ teaspoon cayenne pepper	1
1 (14 ounce) can chicken broth	1 (420 g)
1 (16 ounce) can bean sprouts, drained	1 (454 g)
1 (8 ounce) can water chestnuts, drained	1 (220 g)
1 (6 ounce) can bamboo shoots	1 (180 g)
¼ cup flour	60 mL

- Combine chicken, celery, onion, soy sauce, cayenne pepper and chicken broth in sprayed slow cooker.

- Cover and cook on LOW for 3 to 4 hours.

- Add bean sprouts, water chestnuts and bamboo shoots to chicken.

- Mix flour and ¼ cup (60 mL) water and stir into chicken and vegetables. Cook 1 more hour.

- Serve over chow mein noodles.

Classy Chicken Dinner

1 (6 ounce) box long grain and wild rice	1 (170 g)
12 to 15 frozen chicken breast tenderloins, thawed	12 to 15
1 (16 ounce) jar roasted garlic parmesan cheese creation	1 (454 g)
1 cup frozen petite green peas, thawed	250 mL

- Spray 5-quart (5 L) slow cooker with vegetable cooking spray and pour in 2½ cups (625 mL) water, rice and seasoning packet and stir well.

- Spoon in roasted, garlic parmesan cheese creation and mix well.

- Place chicken tenderloins in slow cooker and cover with green peas.

- Cover and cook on LOW for 4 to 5 hours.

Creamy Chicken and Potatoes

4 boneless, skinless chicken breast halves	4
2 teaspoons chicken seasoning	10 mL
8 to 10 small new potatoes, unpeeled	8 to 10
1 (10 ounce) can cream of chicken soup	1 (284 g)
1 (8 ounce) carton sour cream	1 (225 g)
Black pepper	

- Place chicken breast halves, sprinkled with chicken seasoning, in slow cooker.

- Arrange new potatoes around chicken.

- Combine soup, sour cream and good amount of black pepper. Spoon over chicken breast.

- Cover and cook on LOW for 4 to 6 hours.

Creamed Chicken

4 large boneless, skinless chicken breast halves	4
Lemon juice	
1 sweet red bell pepper, chopped	1
2 ribs celery, sliced diagonally	2
1 (10 ounce) can cream of chicken soup	1 (284 g)
1 (10 ounce) can cream of celery soup	1 (284 g)
1/3 cup dry white wine	75 mL
1 (4 ounce) package shredded parmesan cheese	1 (113 g)

- Wash and pat chicken dry with paper towels, rub a little lemon juice over chicken and sprinkle with salt and pepper.

- Place in slow cooker and top with bell pepper and celery.

- In saucepan, combine soups and wine and heat just enough to mix thoroughly.

- Pour over chicken breasts and sprinkle with parmesan cheese.

- Cover and cook on LOW for 6 to 7 hours. Serve over

Creamed Chicken and Vegetables

4 large boneless, skinless chicken breast halves	**4**
1 (10 ounce) can cream of chicken soup	**1 (284 g)**
1 (16 ounce) package frozen peas and carrots, thawed	**1 (454 g)**
1 (12 ounce) jar chicken gravy	**1 (340 g)**

- Cut chicken in thin slices. Spray 6-quart (6 L) slow cooker with vegetable cooking spray.

- Pour soup and ½ cup (125 mL) water into slow cooker, mix and add chicken slices.

- Sprinkle salt and lots of pepper over chicken and soup.

- Cover and cook on LOW for 4 to 5 hours.

- Add peas, carrots, chicken gravy and another ½ cup (125 mL) water. Increase heat to HIGH and cook for about 1 hour or until peas and carrots are tender.

- Serve over large, refrigerated buttermilk biscuits or over Texas toast (thick slices of bread).

Creamy Salsa Chicken

4 to 5 skinless, boneless skinless chicken breast halves	4 to 5
1 (1 ounce) package dry taco seasoning mix	1 (32 g)
1 cup salsa	250 mL
½ cup sour cream	125 mL

- Spray 5 to 6-quart (6 L) oblong slow cooker with vegetable cooking spray, place chicken breasts in bottom of slow cooker and add ¼ cup (60 mL) water.

- Sprinkle taco seasoning mix over chicken and top with salsa.

- Cook on LOW for 5 to 6 hours.

- When ready to serve, remove chicken breasts and place on platter. Stir sour cream into salsa sauce and spoon over chicken breasts.

Delightful Chicken and Veggies

4 to 5 boneless skinless, chicken breast halves	4 to 5
1 (15 ounce) can whole kernel corn, drained	1 (438 g)
1 (10 ounce) box frozen green peas, thawed	1 (225 g)
1 (16 ounce) jar alfredo sauce	1 (454 g)
1 teaspoon chicken seasoning	5 mL
1 teaspoon prepared minced garlic	5 mL

- Brown chicken breasts in skillet and place in oblong slow cooker sprayed with vegetable cooking spray.

- Combine corn, peas, alfredo sauce, ¼ cup (60 mL) water, chicken seasoning and minced garlic and spoon mixture over chicken breasts.

- Cover and cook on LOW for 4 to 5 hours. Serve over hot cooked pasta.

Slow Cooker Cordon Bleu

4 skinless, boneless chicken breasts halves	**4**
4 slices cooked ham	**4**
4 slices Swiss cheese, softened	**4**
1 (10 ounce) can condensed cream of chicken soup	**1 (284 g)**
¼ cup milk	**60 mL**

- Place chicken breasts on cutting board and pound until breast halves are thin.

- Place ham and cheese slices on chicken breasts, roll up and secure with toothpick.

- Arrange chicken rolls in 4-quart (4 L) slow cooker. Thin chicken soup with milk and pour over chicken rolls.

- Cover and cook on LOW for 4 to 5 hours.

- Serve over hot cooked noodles and cover with sauce from soup.

Delicious Chicken Pasta

1 pound chicken tenders	500 g
Lemon herb chicken seasoning	
3 tablespoons butter	45 mL
1 onion, coarsely chopped	1
1 (15 ounce) can diced tomatoes	1 (438 g)
1 (10 ounce) can golden mushroom soup	1 (284 g)
1 (8 ounce) box angel hair pasta	1 (225 g)

- Pat chicken tenders dry with several paper towels and sprinkle them with lots of chicken seasoning.

- Melt butter in large skillet, brown chicken and place in bottom of oval slow cooker. Pour remaining butter and seasonings over chicken and cover with onion.

- In separate bowl, combine diced tomatoes and mushroom soup and pour over chicken and onions.

- Cover and cook on LOW for 4 to 5 hours.

- When ready to serve, cook pasta according to package directions. Serve chicken and sauce over pasta.

Farmhouse Supper

1 (8 ounce) package uncooked medium noodles	1 (225 g)
4 to 5 chicken breast halves	4 to 5
1 (14 ounce) can chicken broth	1 (420 g)
2 cups sliced celery	500 mL
2 onions, chopped	2
1 green bell pepper, seeded, chopped	1
1 red bell pepper, seeded, chopped	1
1 (10 ounce) can cream of chicken soup	1 (284 g)
1 (10 ounce) can cream of mushroom soup	1 (284 g)
1 cup shredded 4-cheese blend	250 mL

- Cook noodles in boiling water until barely tender and drain well.

- Cut chicken into thin slices.

- In large slow cooker sprayed with vegetable cooking spray, combine noodles, chicken and chicken broth and mix.

- Make sure noodles are separated and coated with broth. Stir in remaining ingredients.

- Cover and cook on LOW for 4 to 6 hours.

Golden Chicken Dinner

6 medium new potatoes, unpeeled, cubed	6
6 medium carrots	6
5 boneless, skinless chicken breast halves	5
1 tablespoon dried parsley flakes	15 mL
1 teaspoon seasoned salt	5 mL
½ teaspoon white pepper	2 mL
1 (10 ounce) can golden mushroom soup	1 (284 g)
1 (10 ounce) can cream of chicken soup	1 (284 g)
4 tablespoons dried mashed potato flakes	60 mL
Water or milk	

- Cut chicken into ½-inch pieces.

- Place potatoes and carrots in slow cooker and top with chicken breasts.

- Sprinkle parsley flakes, seasoned salt and white pepper over chicken. Combine soups and spread over chicken.

- Cover and slow cook on LOW for 6 to 7 hours.

- Stir in potato flakes and a little water or milk if necessary to make gravy and cook another 30 minutes.

Hawaiian Chicken

6 skinless, boneless chicken breast halves	6
1 (15 ounce) can pineapple slices, reserve juice	1 (420 g)
⅓ cup packed brown sugar	75 mL
2 tablespoons lemon juice	30 mL
¼ teaspoon ground ginger	1 mL
¼ cup cornstarch	75 mL

- Place chicken breasts in oblong slow cooker sprayed with vegetable cooking spray and sprinkle with a little salt. Place pineapple slices over chicken.

- In small bowl, combine pineapple juice, brown sugar, lemon juice, ginger and cornstarch and stir until cornstarch mixes with liquids. Pour over chicken breasts.

- Cover and cook on LOW for 4 to 5 hours or on HIGH for 2½ to 3 hours. Serve over hot buttered rice.

Imperial Chicken

1 (6 ounce) box long grain and wild rice	1 (170 g)
6 boneless, skinless chicken breast halves	6
1 (16 ounce) jar roasted garlic parmesan cheese creation	1 (454 g)
1 (16 ounce) box frozen French-style green beans, thawed	1 (454 g)
½ cup slivered almonds, toasted	125 mL

- Spray oblong slow cooker with vegetable cooking spray and pour in 2½ cups (625 mL) water, rice and seasoning packet and stir well.

- Spoon in cheese creation and mix well. Place chicken breasts in slow cooker and cover with green beans.

- Cover and cook on LOW for 3 to 5 hours. When ready to serve, sprinkle with slivered almonds.

Here's the Stuff

5 skinless, boneless chicken breast halves	**5**
2 (10 ounce) cans cream of chicken soup	**1 (284 g)**
1 (6 ounce) box chicken stuffing mix	**1 (170 g)**
1 (16 ounce) package frozen green peas, thawed	**1 (454 g)**

- Place chicken breasts in 6-quart (6 L) slow cooker and spoon soups over chicken.

- Combine stuffing mix with ingredients on package directions, include seasoning packet and spoon over chicken and soup.

- Cover and cook on LOW for 5 to 6 hours.

- Sprinkle drained green peas over top of stuffing. Cover and cook another 45 to 50 minutes.

TIP: Instead of cream of chicken soup, use 1 (10 ounce) (284 g) can cream of chicken soup and 1 (10 ounce) (284 g) can fiesta nacho soup.

Mushroom Chicken

4 boneless, skinless chicken breasts halves	4
1 (15 ounce) can tomato sauce	1 (438 g)
2 (4 ounce) cans sliced mushrooms, drained	1 (125 g)
1 (10 ounce) package frozen seasoning blend onions and peppers	1 (284 g)
2 teaspoons Italian seasoning	10 mL
1 teaspoon prepared minced garlic	5 mL

- In skillet brown chicken breasts and place in oval slow cooker.

- In bowl combine tomato sauce, mushrooms, onions, peppers, Italian seasoning, minced garlic and ¼ cup (50 mL) water and spoon over chicken breasts.

- Cover and cook on LOW for 4 to 5 hours.

Orange Chicken

6 boneless, skinless chicken breasts halves	6
1 (12 ounce) jar orange marmalade	1 (340 g)
1 (8 ounce) bottle Russian dressing	1 (225 g)
1 (1.3 ounce) envelope dry onion soup mix	1 (32 g)

- Place chicken breasts in oblong slow cooker.

- Combine orange marmalade, Russian dressing, onion soup mix and ¾ cup (175 mL) water and stir well. Spoon over chicken breasts.

- Cover and cook on LOW for 4 to 6 hours.

Oregano Chicken

½ cup (1 stick) butter, melted	125 mL
1 (1.3 ounce) envelope dry Italian salad dressing mix	1 (32 g)
1 tablespoon lemon juice	15 mL
4 to 5 boneless, skinless chicken breasts	4 to 5
2 tablespoons dried oregano	30 mL

- In bowl, combine butter, dressing mix and lemon juice and mix well.

- Place chicken breasts in oblong slow cooker sprayed with vegetable cooking spray. Spoon butter-lemon juice mixture over chicken.

- Cover and cook on LOW for 5 to 6 hours.

- One hour before serving, baste chicken with pan liquid and sprinkle oregano over chicken.

Quick-Fix Chicken

4 to 6 boneless, skinless chicken breast halves	4 to 6
1 (8 ounce) carton sour cream	1 (225 g)
¼ cup soy sauce	60 mL
2 (10 ounce) cans French onion soup	2 (284 g)

- Wash and dry chicken with paper towels and place in oblong slow cooker sprayed with vegetable cooking spray.

- Combine sour cream, soy sauce and onion soup, stir and mix well.

- Cover and cook on LOW for 5 to 6 hours if chicken breasts are large, 3 to 4 hours if breasts are medium.

Tip: Serve chicken and sauce with hot, buttered rice or mashed potatoes.

Perfect Chicken Breasts

1 (2.5 ounce) jar dried beef	1 (70 g)
6 small boneless, skinless chicken breast halves	6
6 slices bacon	6
2 (10 ounce) cans golden mushroom soup	2 (284 g)

- Line bottom of oblong slow cooker with slices of dried beef and overlap some.

- Roll each chicken breast with slice of bacon and secure with toothpick. Place in slow-cooker, overlapping as little as possible.

- Combine mushroom soup and ½ cup (125 mL) water or milk and spoon over chicken breasts.

- Cover and cook on LOW for 6 to 8 hours.

When cooked, you will have a great "gravy" that is wonderful served over noodles or rice.

Picante Chicken

4 boneless, skinless chicken breasts	4
1 green bell pepper, seeded, cut in rings	1
1 (16 ounce) jar picante sauce	1 (454 g)
⅓ cup packed brown sugar	75 mL
1 tablespoon prepared mustard	15 mL

- Place chicken breasts in slow cooker with bell pepper rings over top of chicken.

- Combine picante, brown sugar and mustard and spoon over top of chicken.

- Cover and cook on LOW for 4 to 5 hours.

Russian Chicken

1 (8 ounce) bottle Russian salad dressing	1 (225 g)
1 (16 ounce) can whole cranberry sauce	1 (454 g)
1 (1.3 ounce) envelope dry onion soup mix	1 (32 g)
1 chicken, skinned, quartered	1

- In bowl, combine salad dressing, cranberry sauce, ½ cup (125 mL) water and soup mix. Stir well to get all lumps out of soup mix.

- Place 4 chicken pieces in 6-quart (6 L) oval slow cooker. Spoon dressing-cranberry mixture over chicken.

- Cover and cook on LOW for 4 to 5 hours. Serve sauce and chicken over hot cooked rice.

Tip: Use 6 chicken breasts if you don't want to cut-up a chicken.

So-Good Chicken

4 to 5 boneless, skinless chicken breasts	4 to 5
1 (10 ounce) can golden mushroom soup	1 (284 g)
1 cup white cooking wine	250 mL
1 (8 ounce) carton sour cream	1 (227 g)

- Wash, dry chicken breasts with paper towels and sprinkle a little salt and pepper over each.

- In bowl, combine mushroom soup, wine and sour cream and mix well. Spoon over chicken breasts.

- Cover and cook on LOW for 5 to 7 hours.

Winter Dinner

1 pound chicken tenderloins	500 g
1 pound Polish sausage	500 g
2 onions, chopped	2
1 (31 ounce) can pork and beans, liquid reserved	1 (1 kg)
1 (15 ounce) can ranch-style beans, drained	1 (438 g)
1 (15 ounce) can great northern beans	1 (438 g)
1 (15 ounce) can butter beans, drained	1 (438 g)
1 cup ketchup	250 mL
1 cup packed brown sugar	250 mL
1 tablespoon vinegar	15 mL
6 slices bacon, cooked, crumbled	6

- In skillet, brown chicken slices in a little oil and place in large slow cooker sprayed with vegetable cooking spray.

- Add sausage, cut in 1-inch pieces, onions, 4 cans beans, ketchup, brown sugar and vinegar and stir gently.

- Cover and cook on LOW for 7 to 8 hours or on HIGH for 3½ to 4 hours.

- When ready to serve, sprinkle crumbled bacon over top.

Savory Chicken Fettuccine

2 pounds boneless, skinless chicken thighs, cubed	1 kg
½ teaspoon garlic powder	2 mL
½ teaspoon black pepper	2 mL
1 sweet red bell pepper, chopped	1
2 ribs celery, chopped	2
1 (10 ounce) can cream of celery soup	1 (284 g)
1 (10 ounce) can chicken soup	1 (284 g)
1 (8 ounce) package cubed process cheese	1 (225 g)
1 (4 ounce) jar diced pimentos	1 (113 g)
1 (16 ounce) package spinach fettuccine	1 (454 g)

- Place cubed chicken pieces in slow cooker. Sprinkle with garlic powder, black pepper, bell pepper and celery. Top with undiluted soups.

- Cover and cook on HIGH for 4 to 6 hours or until chicken juices are clear.

- Stir in cheese and pimentos. Cover and cook until cheese melts.

- Cook fettuccine according to package directions and drain.

- Place fettuccine in serving bowl and spoon chicken over fettuccine. Serve hot.

Scrumptious Chicken Breasts
There is a lot of delicious sauce.

5 to 6 boneless chicken breast halves	5 to 6
Black pepper	
1 teaspoon chicken seasoning	5 mL
1 (10 ounce) can cream of chicken soup	1 (284 g)
1 (10 ounce) can broccoli-cheese soup	1 (284 g)
½ cup white cooking wine	125 mL

- Spray oval slow cooker with vegetable cooking spray. If chicken breasts are very large, cut them in half lengthwise.

- Place breast halves, sprinkled with black pepper and chicken seasoning, around in cooker.

- In saucepan, combine chicken soup, broccoli-cheese soup and wine. Heat just enough to mix well. Pour over chicken.

- Cover and cook on LOW for 5 to 6 hours.

- Serve chicken and sauce over hot cooked noodles.

Tip: This is great served with roasted garlic, oven-baked Italian toast.

Smothered Chicken Breasts

4 boneless, skinless chicken breast halves	4
1 (10 ounce) can French onion soup	1 (284 g)
½ teaspoon black pepper	2 mL
2 teaspoons chicken seasoning	10 mL
1 (4 ounce) jar sliced mushrooms, drained	1 (113 g)
1 cup shredded mozzarella cheese	250 mL
Chopped green onions	

- In skillet brown each chicken breast and place in oblong slow cooker.

- Pour can of onion soup over chicken and sprinkle black pepper and chicken seasoning over chicken breasts.

- Place mushrooms and cheese over chicken breasts.

- Cover and cook on LOW for 4 to 5 hours.

   Tip: To make this chicken really festive when ready to serve, sprinkle some chopped green onions over each serving.

Southwestern Chicken Pot

6 boneless, skinless chicken breast halves	6
1 teaspoon ground cumin	5 mL
1 teaspoon chili powder	5 mL
1 (10 ounce) can cream of chicken soup	1 (284 g)
1 (10 ounce) can fiesta nacho cheese soup	1 (284 g)
1 cup salsa	250 mL

- In oblong slow cooker sprayed with vegetable cooking spray, place chicken breasts sprinkled with cumin, chili powder and some salt and pepper.

- In saucepan, combine chicken soup, nacho cheese soup and salsa, heat just enough to mix and pour over chicken breasts.

- Cover and cook on LOW for 6 to 7 hours.

- Serve over hot cooked rice with warmed flour tortillas spread with butter.

Sweet and Sour Chicken

6 boneless, skinless chicken breasts	6
Oil	
1 (1.3 ounce) envelope dry onion soup mix	1 (32 g)
1 (6 ounce) can frozen orange juice concentrate, thawed	1 (170 g)

- In skillet, brown chicken breasts in little oil and place in large slow cooker sprayed with vegetable cooking spray.

- In bowl, combine onion soup mix, orange juice concentrate and ½ cup (125 mL) water and pour over chicken.

- Cover and cook on LOW for 3 to 5 hours.

Sunday Chicken

4 large boneless, skinless chicken breast halves	4
Chicken seasoning	
4 slices American cheese	4
1 (10 ounce) can cream of celery soup	1 (284 g)
½ cup sour cream	125 mL
1 (6 ounce) box chicken stuffing mix	1 (170 g)
½ cup (1 stick) butter, melted	125 mL

- Wash, dry chicken breasts with paper towels and place in oval slow cooker. Sprinkle each breast with chicken seasoning.

- Place slice of cheese over each chicken breast.

- Combine celery soup and sour cream, mix well and spoon over chicken and cheese.

- Sprinkle chicken stuffing mix over top of cheese. Drizzle melted butter over stuffing mix.

- Cover and cook on LOW for 5 to 6 hours.

Tasty Chicken-Rice and Veggies

4 boneless, skinless chicken breast halves	4
2 (10 ounce) jars sweet and sour sauce	1 (284 g)
1 (16 ounce) package frozen broccoli, cauliflower and carrots, thawed	1 (454 g)
1 (10 ounce) package frozen baby peas, thawed	1 (284 g)
2 cups sliced celery	500 mL
1 (6.2 ounce) package parmesan and butter-rice mix	1 (170 g)
⅓ cup toasted, slivered almonds	75 mL

- Cut chicken in 1-inch strips.

- Combine pieces, sweet and sour sauce and all vegetables in 6-quart (6 L) slow cooker sprayed with vegetable cooking spray.

- Cover and cook on LOW for 4 to 6 hours.

- When ready to serve cook parmesan-butter rice according to directions on package and fold in almonds.

- Serve chicken and vegetables over hot cooked rice.

Honey-Baked Chicken

2 small fryer chickens, quartered	2
½ cup (1 stick) butter, melted	125 mL
⅔ cup honey	150 mL
¼ cup Dijon mustard	60 mL
1 teaspoon curry powder	5 mL

- Place chicken pieces in large slow cooker, skin side up and sprinkle a little salt over chicken.

- In bowl, combine butter, honey, mustard and curry powder and mix well.

- Pour butter-mustard mixture over chicken quarters.

- Cover and cook on LOW for 6 to 8 hours. Baste chicken once during cooking.

Tangy Chicken

1 large fryer-broiler chicken, quartered	1
2 tablespoons (¼ stick) butter	30 mL
½ cup Heinz 57 sauce	125 mL
1 (15 ounce) can stewed tomatoes	1 (438 g)

- Wash, dry chicken quarters with paper towels and place in large slow cooker.

- In saucepan, combine butter, 57 sauce and stewed tomatoes. Heat just until butter melts and ingredients mix well. Pour over chicken.

- Cover and cook on LOW for 5 to 6 hours.

Chicken with Orange Sauce

1 whole chicken, quartered	1
½ cup plus 2 tablespoons flour	125 mL
½ teaspoon ground nutmeg	2 mL
½ teaspoon cinnamon	2 mL
2 large sweet potatoes, peeled, sliced	2
1 (8 ounce) can pineapple chunks, liquid reserved	1 (225 g)
1 (10 ounce) can cream of chicken soup	1 (284 g)
⅔ cup orange juice	150 mL

- Wash and dry chicken quarters with paper towels.

- In bowl combine ½ cup (125 mL) flour, nutmeg and cinnamon.

- Coat chicken with flour mixture.

- Place sweet potatoes and pineapple in bottom of large slow cooker sprayed with vegetable cooking spray. Arrange chicken on top.

- In bowl, combine chicken soup, orange juice and remaining flour and pour over chicken.

- Cover and cook on LOW for 7 to 9 hours or on HIGH for 3 to 4 hours. Serve over hot buttered rice.

Tasty Chicken and Veggies

1 (2½ to 3 pound) whole chicken, quartered	1 (1 to 1.5 kg)
1 (16 ounce) package baby carrots	1 (450 g)
4 potatoes, peeled, sliced	4
3 ribs celery, sliced	3
1 onion, peeled, sliced	1
1 cup Italian salad dressing	250 mL
⅔ cup chicken broth	150 mL

- Rinse, dry and place chicken quarters in sprayed 6-quart (6 L) slow cooker with carrots, potatoes, celery and onion.

- Pour salad dressing and chicken broth over chicken and vegetables.

- Cover and cook on LOW for 6 to 8 hours.

   Tip: When serving, garnish with sprigs of fresh parsley.

"Baked" Chicken

1 cup uncooked white rice	250 mL
2 (10 ounce) cans cream of chicken soup	2 (284 g)
1 (14 ounce) can chicken broth	1 (420 g)
1 (1.3 ounce) envelope dry onion soup mix	1 (32 g)
1 chicken, quartered	1

- Place rice in 5 to 6-quart (6 L) oval slow cooker.

- In saucepan, combine chicken soup, broth, 2 soup cans water (500 mL) and onion soup mix and mix well. Heat just enough to mix ingredients.

- Spoon half over rice and place 4 chicken quarters in slow cooker. Spoon remaining soup mixture over chicken.

- Cover and cook on LOW for 5 to 6 hours.

Saffron Rice and Chicken

1 fryer-broiler chicken, quartered	1
½ teaspoon garlic powder	2 mL
1 (14 ounce) can chicken broth	1 (420 g)
1 onion, chopped	1
1 green bell pepper, chopped	1
1 yellow bell pepper, chopped	1
1 (4 ounce) jar pimentos, drained	1 (113 g)
⅓ cup prepared bacon bits	75 mL
2 tablespoons (¼ stick) butter, melted	30 mL
1 (5 ounce) package saffron yellow rice mix	1 (140 g)

- Sprinkle chicken with garlic powder, salt and pepper.

- In skillet, brown chicken quarters in little oil.

- Place chicken in oblong slow cooker sprayed with vegetable cooking spray and pour broth in slow cooker.

- Combine, onion, bell peppers, pimentos and bacon bits and spoon over chicken quarters.

- Cover and cook on LOW for 4 to 5 hours.

- Carefully remove chicken quarters from cooker, stir in rice mix and butter and return chicken to cooker.

- Cover and cook 1 hour or until rice is tender.

Lemon Chicken

1 (2½ to 3 pound) chicken, quartered	1 (1 to 1.5 kg)
1 teaspoon dried oregano	5 mL
2 teaspoons prepared minced garlic	10 mL
2 tablespoons (¼ stick) butter	30 mL
¼ cup lemon juice	60 mL

- Season chicken quarters with salt, pepper and oregano and rub garlic on chicken.

- In skillet, brown chicken quarters on all sides in butter and transfer to oblong slow cooker sprayed with vegetable cooking spray.

- Add ⅓ cup (75 mL) water to skillet, scrape bottom and pour over chicken

- Cover and cook on LOW for 6 to 8 hours.

- At last hour of cooking, pour lemon juice over chicken, finish cooking.

Chicken Coq Vin

1 large broiler-fryer, quartered	1
Oil	
10 to 12 small white onions, peeled	10 to 12
½ pound whole mushrooms	227 g
1 teaspoon prepared minced garlic	5 mL
½ teaspoon dried thyme leaves	2 mL
10 to 12 small new potatoes, unpeeled	10 to 12
1 (10 ounce) can chicken broth	1 (284 g)
1 cup burgundy wine	250 mL
6 bacon slices, cooked, crumbled	6

- In skillet, brown chicken quarters on both sides and set aside.

- Place white onions, whole mushrooms, garlic and thyme in oblong slow cooker.

- Add chicken quarters, potatoes chicken broth and a little salt and pepper.

- Cover and cook on LOW for 8 to 10 hours or on HIGH for 3 to 4 hours.

- During last hour, turn heat to HIGH, add burgundy and continue cooking.

- Sprinkle crumbled bacon over chicken before serving.

Chicken Cacciatore

2 onions, thinly sliced	2
1 (2½ to 3) pound fryer chicken, quartered	1 (1 to 1.5 kg)
2 (6 ounce) cans tomato paste	2 (180 g)
1 (4 ounce) can sliced mushrooms	1 (113 g)
1½ teaspoons prepared minced garlic	7 mL
½ teaspoon dried basil	2 mL
2 teaspoons oregano leaves	10 mL
⅔ cup dry white wine	150 mL

- Place sliced onions in oblong slow cooker sprayed with vegetable cooking spray.

- Wash, dry chicken quarters with paper towels and place in slow cooker.

- In bowl, combine tomato paste, mushrooms, garlic, basil, oregano and wine and pour over chicken quarters.

- Cover and cook on LOW for 7 to 8 hours or on HIGH for 4 hours.

Taco Chicken

3 cups chopped chicken	750 mL
1 (1.3 ounce) envelope taco seasoning	1 (32 g)
1 cup uncooked white rice	250 mL
2 cups chopped celery	500 mL
1 green bell pepper, seeded, chopped	1
2 (15 ounce) cans Mexican stewed tomatoes	2 (438 g)

- Combine chicken, taco seasoning, rice, celery, bell pepper and stewed tomatoes and mix well. Pour into 5-quart (5 L) slow cooker.

- Cover and cook on LOW for 4 to 5 hours.

Tip: This is a great recipe for leftover chicken.

Monterey Bake

6 (6-inch) corn tortillas	6 (15 cm)
3 cups leftover chicken, cubed	750 mL
1 (10 ounce) package frozen whole kernel corn	1 (284 g)
1 (15 ounce) can pinto beans, liquid reserved	1 (438 g)
1 (16 ounce) hot jar salsa	1 (454 g)
¼ cup sour cream	60 mL
1 tablespoon flour	15 mL
3 tablespoons snipped fresh cilantro	45 mL
1 (8 ounce) package shredded 4-cheese blend	1 (227 g)

- Cut tortillas into 6 wedges.

- In bottom of slow cooker sprayed with vegetable cooking spray, place half wedges of tortillas.

- Place remaining wedges on cooking sheet, bake about 10 minutes at 350° (176° C) and set aside.

- Layer chicken, corn and beans over tortillas in cooker.

- In bowl combine salsa, sour cream, flour and cilantro and pour over corn and beans.

- Cover and cook on LOW for 3 to 4 hours.

- When ready to serve, place cheese and baked tortillas wedges on top of each serving.

Chicken and Stuffing

1 (10 ounce) can cream of chicken soup	1 (284 g)
2 ribs celery, sliced	2
½ cup (1 stick) butter, melted	125 mL
3 cups cooked cubed chicken	750 mL
1 (16 ounce) package frozen broccoli, corn and red peppers	1 (454 g)
1 (8 ounce) box cornbread stuffing mix	1 (227 g)

- In large mixing bowl, combine chicken soup, celery, butter, cubed chicken, vegetables, stuffing mix and ⅓ cup (75 mL) water.

- Mix well and transfer to 5 or 6-quart (6 L) slow cooker.

- Cover and cook on LOW for 5 to 6 hours.

Tip: This is a great recipe for leftover chicken.

Chicken and Everything Good

2 (10 ounce) cans cream of chicken soup	2 (284 g)
5 tablespoons (⅔ stick) butter, melted	75 mL
3 cups cooked, cubed chicken	750 mL
1 (16 ounce) package frozen broccoli, corn and red peppers	1 (454 g)
1 (10 ounce) package frozen green peas	1 (284 g)
1 (8 ounce) package cornbread stuffing mix	1 (227 g)

- Spray large slow cooker with vegetable cooking spray.

- In mixing bowl, combine soup, melted butter and ⅓ cup (75 mL) water and mix well.

- Add chicken, vegetables and stuffing mix and stir well. Spoon into cooker.

- Cover and cook on LOW for 5 to 6 hours or on HIGH for 2½ to 3 hours.

Chicken Alfredo

1½ pounds boneless chicken thighs, cut into strips	750 g
2 ribs celery, sliced diagonally	2
1 sweet red bell pepper, julienned	1
1 (16 ounce) jar alfredo sauce	1 (454 g)
3 cups fresh broccoli florets	750 mL
1 (8 ounce) package fettuccine or linguine	1 (227 g)
1 (4 ounce) package shredded parmesan cheese	1 (113 g)

- Cut chicken into strips.

- In 4 or 5-quart (5 L) slow cooker, layer chicken, celery and bell pepper.

- Pour alfredo sauce evenly over vegetables.

- Cover and cook on LOW for 5 to 6 hours.

- About 30 minutes before serving, turn heat to HIGH and add broccoli florets to chicken-alfredo mixture.

- Cover and cook another 30 minutes.

- Cook pasta according to package directions and drain.

- Just before serving pour pasta into cooker, mix and sprinkle parmesan cheese on top.

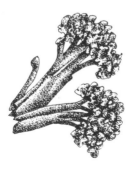

Sweet and Spicy Chicken

2 pounds chicken thighs	1 kg
¾ cup chili sauce	175 mL
¾ cup packed brown sugar	175 mL
1 (1.3 ounce) envelope dry onion soup mix	1 (32 g)
⅛ teaspoon cayenne pepper	½ mL

- Spray 5-quart (5 L) slow cooker with vegetable cooking spray and arrange chicken pieces in bottom of cooker.

- Combine chili sauce, brown sugar, dry onion soup mix, cayenne pepper and ¼ cup (60 mL) water and spoon over chicken

- Cover and cook on LOW for 6 to 7 hours. Serve over hot, cooked rice.

Maple-Plum Glazed Turkey Breast

1 cup red plum jam	250 mL
1 cup maple syrup	250 mL
1 teaspoon dry mustard	5 mL
¼ cup lemon juice	60 mL
1 (3 to 5 pound) bone-in turkey breast	1 (1.5 to 2 kg)

- In saucepan, combine jam, syrup, mustard and lemon juice. Bring to boiling, turn heat down and simmer about 20 minutes or until slightly thick. Reserve 1 cup (250 mL).

- Place turkey breast in slow cooker and pour remaining glaze over turkey.

- Cover and cook on LOW for 5 to 7 hours.

- When ready to serve, slice turkey and serve with heated, reserved glaze.

Southern Chicken

1 cup half-and-half cream	250 mL
1 tablespoon flour	15 mL
1 (1.2 ounce) envelope chicken gravy mix	1 (32 g)
1 pound boneless chicken thighs	500 g
1 (16 ounce) package frozen stew vegetables, thawed	1 (454 g)
1 (4 ounce) jar sliced mushrooms, drained	1 (113 g)
1 (10 ounce) package frozen green peas, thawed	1 (284 g)
1½ cups biscuit baking mix	375 mL
1 bunch fresh green onions, chopped	1
½ cup milk	125 mL

- In bowl, combine cream, flour, gravy mix and 1 cup (250 mL) water, stir until smooth and pour in large slow cooker.

- Cut chicken into 1-inch pieces and stir in vegetables and mushrooms.

- Cover and cook on LOW for 4 to 6 hours or until chicken is tender and sauce thickens. Stir in peas.

- In bowl, combine baking mix, onions and milk and mix well.

- Drop dough by tablespoonfuls onto chicken mixture.

- Change heat to HIGH, cover and cook another 50 to 60 minutes.

Italian Chicken

1 small head cabbage	1
1 onion	1
1 (4 ounce) jar sliced mushrooms, drained	1 (113 g)
1 medium zucchini, sliced	1
1 sweet red bell pepper, julienned	1
1 teaspoon Italian seasoning	5 mL
1½ pounds chicken thighs, skinned	750 g
2 (15 ounce) cans Italian stewed tomatoes	2 (438 g)
1 teaspoon minced garlic	5 mL

- Spray 6-quart (6 L) slow cooker with vegetable cooking spray.

- Cut cabbage into wedges, slice onions and separate into rings.

- Make layers of cabbage, mushrooms, onion, zucchini and bell pepper in bottom of cooker.

- Sprinkle Italian seasoning over vegetables. Place chicken thighs on top of vegetables.

- Mix garlic with tomatoes and pour over chicken.

- Cover and cook on LOW for 4 to 6 hours.

Tip: When serving, sprinkle a little parmesan cheese over each serving.

Asparagus-Cheese Chicken

8 to 10 chicken thighs, skinned	8 to 10
2 tablespoons (¼ stick) butter	30 mL
1 (10 ounce) can cream of celery soup	1 (284 g)
1 (10 ounce) can cheddar cheese soup	1 (284 g)
⅓ cup milk	75 mL
1 (16 ounce) package frozen asparagus cuts	1 (454 g)

- Place chicken thighs in 5-quart (5 L) slow cooker.

- In saucepan, combine butter, celery soup, cheddar cheese soup and milk. Heat just enough for butter to melt and mix well. Pour over chicken thighs.

- Cover and cook on LOW for 5 to 6 hours.

- Remove cover and place asparagus cuts over chicken and cook 1 hour more.

Arroz Con Pollo

3 pounds chicken thighs	3
2 (15 ounce) cans Italian stewed tomatoes	2 (438 g)
1 (16 ounce) package frozen green peas, thawed	1 (454 g)
2 cups uncooked long-grain rice	500 mL
1 (.28 ounce) package yellow rice seasoning mix	1 (8 g)
2 (14 ounce) can chicken broth	2 (420 g)
1 heaping teaspoon prepared minced garlic	5 mL
1 teaspoon dried oregano	5 mL

- In large slow cooker sprayed with vegetable cooking spray, combine all ingredients plus ¾ cup (175 mL) water and stir well.

- Cover and cook on LOW for 7 to 8 hours or on HIGH for 3½ to 4 hours.

Turkey Bake

1½ pounds turkey tenderloins	750 g
1 (6.2 ounce) package Oriental rice and vermicelli	1 (170 g)
1 (10 ounce) package frozen green peas, thawed	1 (284 g)
1 cup sliced celery	250 mL
4 tablespoons (¼ stick) butter, melted	60 mL
1 (14 ounce) can chicken broth	1 (420 g)
1½ cups fresh broccoli florets	375 mL

- Cut tenderloins in strips.

- In non-stick skillet, saute turkey strips until no longer pink.

- In large slow cooker, combine turkey strips, rice-vermicelli mix plus seasoning packet, peas, celery, butter, chicken broth and 1 cup (250 mL) water and mix well.

- Cover and cook on LOW for 4 to 5 hours.

- Turn heat to HIGH setting, add broccoli and cook another 20 minutes.

Turkey Cassoulet

2 cups cooked turkey, cubed	500 mL
8 ounces smoked turkey sausage	227 g
3 carrots, sliced	3
1 onion, halved, sliced	1
1 (15 ounce) can navy bean	1 (438 g)
1 (15 ounce) can white lima beans	1 (438 g)
1 (8 ounce) can tomato sauce	1 (227 g)
1 teaspoon dried thyme	5 mL
¼ teaspoon ground allspice	1 mL

- Cut turkey sausage in ½-inch pieces.

- Combine all ingredients in slow cooker sprayed with vegetable cooking spray.

- Cover and cook on LOW for 4 to 5 hours.

Tip: This is a great recipe for leftover turkey

Tangy Chicken Legs

12 to 15 chicken legs	12 to 15
⅓ cup soy sauce	75 mL
⅔ cup packed brown sugar	150 mL
Scant ⅛ teaspoon ground ginger	.5 mL

- Place chicken legs in 5-quart (5 L) slow cooker.

- Combine soy sauce, brown sugar, ¼ cup (60 mL) water and ginger and spoon over chicken legs.

- Cover and cook on LOW for 4 to 5 hours.

Turkey Loaf

2 pounds ground turkey	1 kg
1 onion, very finely chopped	1
½ sweet red bell pepper, very finely chopped	½
2 teaspoons prepared minced garlic	10 mL
½ cup chili sauce	125 mL
2 large eggs, beaten	2
½ teaspoon black pepper	2 mL
¾ cup Italian seasoned dry breadcrumbs	175 mL

- Make foil handles by cutting three 18x3-inch strips of heavy foil; place in bottom of slow cooker in crisscross strips (resembles spokes on wheel) up and over sides. Fold extended strips over food. When finished cooking lift food out by handles.

- In large bowl, combine all ingredients plus 1 teaspoon (5 mL) salt and mix well.

- Shape into round loaf and place on top of foil handles.

- Cover and cook on LOW for 5 to 6 hours.

Turkey and Spaghetti

2 pounds ground turkey	1 kg
2 (10 ounce) cans tomato bisque soup	2 (284 g)
1 (14 ounce) can chicken broth	1 (420 g)
2 (7 ounce) boxes ready-cut spaghetti, cooked, drained	2 (200 g)
1 (15 ounce) can whole kernel corn, drained	1 (438 g)
1 (4 ounce) can sliced mushrooms, drained	1 (125 g)
¼ cup ketchup	60 mL

- In non-stick skillet, brown, cook ground turkey and season with salt and pepper.

- Place in 5 or 6-quart (6 L) slow cooker.

- Add soups, broth, spaghetti, corn, mushrooms, ketchup, and stir to blend.

- Cover and cook on LOW for 5 to 7 hours or on HIGH for 3 hours.

Colorful Rice and Turkey

1 (10 ounce) can cream of mushroom	1 (284 g)
1 (10 ounce) can cream of chicken soup	1 (284 g)
2 cups white rice	500 mL
3 ribs celery, sliced diagonally	3
1 (16 ounce) package frozen Oriental vegetable mix, frozen	1 (454 g)
3 cups cooked, cubed turkey or chicken	750 mL
1 teaspoon poultry seasoning	5 mL
2 (14 ounce) cans chicken broth	2 (420 g)

- In 5 or 6-quart (6 L) slow cooker sprayed with vegetable cooking spray, place all ingredients plus 1 soup can (284 g) water and stir well.

- Cover and cook on LOW for 5 to 6 hours.

Sausage and Rice

1 pound turkey sausage	500 g
1 (6 ounce) box flavored rice mix	1 (170 g)
2 (14 ounce) cans chicken broth	2 (420 g)
2 cups sliced celery	500 mL
1 sweet red bell pepper, julienned	1
1 (15 ounce) can cut green beans, drained	1 (438 g)
⅓ cup toasted slivered almonds	75 mL

- Break up turkey sausage up and brown in skillet.

- Place in 4 to 5-quart (5 L) slow cooker.

- Add rice, 1 cup (250 mL) water, chicken broth, celery, bell pepper and green beans and stir to mix.

- Cover and cook on LOW for 3 to 4 hours.

- When ready to serve, sprinkle almonds over top of cooker.

BEEF

Savory Steak

Great sauce with mashed potatoes

1½ pounds lean round steak	750 g
1 teaspoon pepper	5 mL
1 onion, halved, sliced	1
2 (10 ounce) cans golden mushroom soup	2 (284 g)
1½ cups hot, thick and chunky salsa	375 mL

- Trim fat from steak and cut into serving-size pieces.

- Sprinkle with pepper and place in 5 to 6-quart (6 L) slow cooker sprayed with vegetable cooking spray.

- Place onion slices over steak.

- Combine mushroom soup and salsa and mix well. Spoon over steak and onions.

- Cover and cook on LOW for 7 to 8 hours.

Pepper Steak

1½ pounds round steak	750 g
¼ cup soy sauce	60 mL
1 onion, sliced	1
1 teaspoon prepared minced garlic	5 mL
1 teaspoon sugar	5 mL
¼ teaspoon ground ginger	1 mL
1 (15 ounce) can stewed tomatoes	1 (438 g)
2 green bell peppers, julienned	2
1 teaspoon beef bouillon	5 mL
1 tablespoon cornstarch	15 mL

- Slice beef in strips, brown in skillet with small amount of oil and place in oblong slow cooker.

- Add soy sauce, onion, garlic, sugar and ginger and spoon over beef.

- Cover and cook on LOW for 5 to 6 hours.

- Add tomatoes and green peppers and bouillon and cook 1 hour more.

- Combine cornstarch and ¼ cup water (60 ml) and stir into cooker.

- Continue cooking until liquid thickens.

- Serve over hot buttered rice or noodles.

Swiss Steak

1 to 1½ pounds boneless, round steak	500 to 750 g
½ teaspoon seasoned salt	2 mL
½ teaspoon seasoned pepper	2 mL
8 to 10 medium new (red) potatoes, unpeeled, halved	8 to 10
1 cup baby carrots	250 mL
1 onion, sliced	1
1 (15 ounce) can stewed tomatoes	1 (438 g)
1 (12 ounce) jar beef gravy	1 (340 g)

- Cut steak in 6 to 8 serving-size pieces, season with seasoned salt and pepper and brown in non-stick skillet.

- Layer steak pieces, potatoes, carrots and onion in slow cooker.

- In bowl, combine tomatoes and beef gravy and spoon over vegetables.

- Cover and cook on LOW for 7 to 8 hours.

Spicy Swiss Steak

1½ pounds boneless, beef round steak	750 g
4 ounces spicy bratwurst	113 g
2 small onions	2
2 tablespoons quick-cooking tapioca	30 mL
1 teaspoon dried thyme	5 mL
2 (15 ounce) cans Mexican stewed tomatoes	2 (438 g)

- Trim fat from steak and cut into 4 serving-size pieces.

- In skillet, brown steak and bratwurst. Drain and place in sprayed 4 to 5-quart (5 L) slow cooker.

- Slice onions and separate into rings.

- Cover meat with onions and sprinkle with tapioca, thyme, a little salt and pepper. Pour stewed tomatoes over onion and seasonings.

- Cover and cook on LOW for 5 to 8 hours.

- Serve over hot cooked noodles.

Stroganoff

2 pounds beef round steak	1 kg
¾ cup flour, divided	175 mL
½ teaspoon prepared mustard	2 mL
2 onions, thinly sliced	2
½ pound fresh mushrooms, sliced	250 g
1 (10 ounce) can beef broth	1 (284 g)
¼ cup dry white wine or cooking wine	60 mL
1 (8 ounce) carton sour cream	1 (227 g)

- Trim excess fat from steak and cut into 3-inch strips about ½-inch wide.

- In bowl, combine ½ cup (125 mL) flour, mustard and a little salt and pepper and toss with steak strips.

- Place strips in oblong slow cooker sprayed with vegetable cooking spray.

- Cover with onions and mushrooms. Add beef broth and wine.

- Cover and cook on LOW for 8 to 10 hours.

- Just before serving, combine sour cream and ¼ cup (60 mL) flour.

- Stir into cooker and cook another 10 to 15 minutes or until stroganoff thickens slightly.

Teriyaki Steak

1½ to 2 pounds flank steak	750 g to 1 kg
1 (15 ounce) can sliced pineapple, liquid reserved	1 (438 g)
1 tablespoon white wine worcestershire sauce	15 mL
⅓ cup packed brown sugar	75 mL
3 tablespoons soy sauce	45 mL
½ teaspoon ground ginger	2 mL
1 (14 ounce) can chicken broth	1 (420 g)
1 cup uncooked long-grain converted rice	250 mL

- Roll flank steak, tie and cut into 7 to 8 individual steaks.

- In bowl large enough for marinade to cover individual steaks, combine ½ cup (125 mL) pineapple juice, worcestershire, sugar, soy sauce and ginger.

- Marinate steaks for 1 hour in juice-soy sauce mixture.

- Pour chicken broth into slow cooker sprayed with vegetable cooking spray.

- Add rice and ¾ cup (175 mL) water. Place steaks over rice and broth.

- Cover and cook on LOW for 8 to 10 hours.

Mushroom-Round Steak

1½ to 2 pounds round steak	750 g to 1 kg
1 (1.3 ounce) envelope dry onion soup mix	1 (32 g)
½ cup dry red wine	125 mL
1 (8 ounce) container fresh mushrooms, sliced	1 (225 g)
1 (10 ounce) can French onion soup	1 (284 g)

- Cut round steak in serving-size pieces and place in oblong slow cooker sprayed with vegetable cooking spray.

- Combine soup mix, red wine, mushrooms, French onion soup and ½ cup (125 mL) water; spoon over steak pieces.

- Cover and cook on LOW for 7 to 8 hours.

O'Brian's Hash

3 cups cubed, cooked beef roast	750 mL
1 (28 ounce) package frozen hash browns with onions and peppers, thawed	1 (800 g)
1 (16 ounce) jar salsa	1 (454 g)
1 tablespoon beef seasoning	15 mL
1 cup shredded cheddar-jack cheese	250 mL

- In large slow cooker sprayed with vegetable cooking spray, place cubed beef.

- Brown potatoes in little oil in large skillet and transfer to slow cooker. Stir in salsa and beef seasoning.

- Cover and cook on HIGH for 4 to 5 hours.

- When ready to serve, sprinkle cheese over hash.

Italian Steak

1 pound round steak	500 g
2 cups fresh mushrooms, halved	500 mL
1 (15 ounce) can Italian stewed tomatoes	1 (438 g)
1 (10 ounce) can beef broth	1 (284 g)
½ cup red wine	125 mL
2 teaspoons Italian seasoning	10 mL
3 tablespoons quick-cooking tapioca	45 mL

- Cut steak into 1-inch cubes.

- Place beef in 4 to 5-quart (5 L) slow cooker sprayed with vegetable cooking spray.

- Add mushrooms, Italian tomatoes, beef broth, wine, Italian seasoning, tapioca and salt and pepper, if desired.

- Cover and cook on LOW for 8 to 10 hours.

- Serve over hot, buttered linguine.

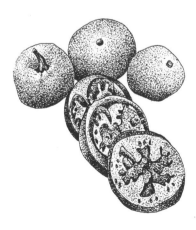

Beefy Onion Supper

1 to 1½ pounds round steak	500 to 750 g
1 onion	1
2 cups fresh sliced mushrooms	500 mL
1 (10 ounce) can French onion soup	1 (284 g)
1 (6 ounce) package herb stuffing mix	1 (170 g)
½ cup (1 stick) butter, melted	125 mL

- Cut beef into 5 to 6 serving-size pieces.

- Slice onion and separate into rings.

- In oblong slow cooker, place steak pieces and top with mushrooms and onions.

- Pour soup over ingredients in cooker.

- Cover and cook on LOW for 7 to 9 hours.

- Just before serving, combine stuffing mix, seasoning packet, butter plus ½ cup (125 mL) liquid from cooker and toss to mix.

- Place stuffing mixture on top of steak and increase heat to HIGH .

- Cover and cook additional 15 minutes or until stuffing is fluffy.

Beef Roulades

1½ pounds beef flank steak	750 g
5 slices bacon	5
¾ cup finely chopped onion	175 mL
1 (4 ounce) can mushrooms pieces	1 (113 g)
1 tablespoon worcestershire	15 mL
⅓ cup Italian dry, seasoned breadcrumbs	75 mL
1 (12 ounce) jar beef gravy	1 (340 g)

- Cut steak into 4 to 6 serving-size pieces.

- With kitchen shears, cut bacon into small pieces and combine with onion, mushrooms, worcestershire and breadcrumbs.

- Place about ½ cup (125 mL) mixture on each piece of meat.

- Roll up meat and secure ends with wooden picks. Dry beef rolls with paper towels.

- In skillet, brown rolled up pieces of meat and transfer to slow cooker sprayed with vegetable cooking spray.

- Pour gravy evenly over steaks to thoroughly moisten.

- Cover and cook on LOW for 7 to 9 hours.

Tip: This is good served with mashed potatoes.

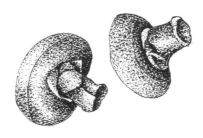

Beef Tips Over Noodles

½ cup plus 3 tablespoons flour, divided	170 mL
3 pounds beef tips	1.5 kg
½ pound fresh mushrooms, sliced	250 g
1 bunch fresh green onions, chopped	1
1 small sweet red bell pepper, chopped	1
¼ cup ketchup	60 mL
1 (14 ounce) can beef broth	1 (420 g)
1 tablespoon worcestershire sauce	15 mL

- In bowl, coat beef tips with ½ cup (125 mL) flour and transfer to slow cooker sprayed with vegetable cooking spray.

- Add mushrooms, onion, bell pepper, ketchup, beef broth, worcestershire and salt and pepper to taste.

- Cover and cook on LOW for 8 to 9 hours. About 1 hour before serving, turn heat to HIGH.

- In small bowl, combine remaining flour with ¼ cup (60 mL) water, stir into cooker and cook until liquid thickens.

- Serve over hot buttered noodles.

Beef Tips Over Pasta

2 to 2½ pounds lean, beef stew meat	1 to 1.25 kg
2 cups frozen, small whole onions, thawed	500 mL
1 (6 ounce) jar pitted Greek olives or ripe olives	1 (100 g)
½ cup sun-dried tomatoes in oil, drained, chopped	125 mL
1 green bell pepper, seeded	1
1 (28 ounce) jar marinara sauce	1 (800 g)
1 (8 ounce) package pasta twirls, cooked	1 (227 g)

- In sprayed 4 or 5-quart (5 L) slow cooker, place beef and onions.

- Cut bell pepper in 1-inch cubes and add to slow cooker.

- Add olives, tomatoes and bell pepper and pour marinara sauce over top.

- Cover and cook on LOW for 8 to 10 hours.

- Serve over hot pasta twirls.

Pot Roast and Veggies

1 (2 pound) chuck roast	1 (1 kg)
4 to 5 medium potatoes, peeled, quartered	4 to 5
4 large carrots	4
1 onion, quartered	1
1 (14 ounce) can beef broth	1 (420 g)
2 tablespoons cornstarch	30 mL

- Trim fat from pieces of roast. Cut roast into 2 equal pieces.

- In skillet, brown pieces of roast (if desired, coat roast pieces with flour, salt and pepper).

- Spray 4 to 5-quart (5 L) slow cooker with vegetable cooking spray.

- Place potatoes, carrots and onion in slow cooker and mix well.

- Place browned beef over vegetables.

- Pour 1½ cups (375 mL) beef broth over beef and veggies.

- Reserve and chill remaining broth.

- Cover and cook on LOW for 8 to 9 hours.

- About 5 minutes before serving, remove beef and veggies with slotted spoon and place on serving platter (cover to keep warm).

- Pour liquid from slow cooker into medium saucepan.

- In small bowl, blend remaining ½ cup (125 mL) broth and cornstarch until smooth and add to liquid in saucepan.

- Boil 1 minute and stir constantly.

- Serve gravy with roast and veggies. Season with salt and pepper if desired.

Sweet and Sour Beef

1 (2 pound) boneless chuck roast	1 (1 kg)
½ cup flour	125 mL
Salt and pepper to taste	
Oil	
1 onion, sliced	1
½ cup chili sauce	125 mL
¾ cup packed brown sugar	175 mL
¼ cup red wine vinegar	60 mL
1 tablespoon worcestershire sauce	15 mL
1 (16 ounce) package peeled baby carrots	1 (454 g)

- Cut beef into 1-inch cubes and dredge in flour, salt and pepper.

- In skillet, brown beef in a little oil and place in slow cooker.

- Add remaining ingredients, except carrots, and 1 cup (250 mL) water.

- Cover and cook on LOW for 7 to 8 hours.

- Add carrots and cook 1½ hours.

Old-Time Pot Roast

1 (2 to 2½) pound boneless rump roast	1 (1 to 1.5 kg)
5 medium potatoes, peeled, quartered	5
1 (16 ounce) package peeled baby carrots	1 (454 g)
2 medium onions, quartered	2
1 (10 ounce) can golden mushroom soup	1 (284 g)
½ teaspoon dried basil	2 mL
½ teaspoon seasoned salt	2 mL

- In skillet lightly coated with vegetable cooking spray, brown roast on all sides.

- Place potatoes, carrots and onions in 4 to 5-quart (5 L) slow cooker sprayed with vegetable cooking spray.

- Place browned roast on top of vegetables.

- In bowl, combine soup, basil and seasoned salt and pour over meat and vegetables

- Cover and cook on LOW for 9 to 11 hours.

Tip: To serve, transfer roast and vegetables to serving plate. Stir juices remaining in slow cooker and spoon over roast and vegetables.

Beef Tips and Mushroom Supreme

2 (10 ounce) cans golden mushroom soup	1 (284 g)
1 (14 ounce) can beef broth	1 (420 g)
1 tablespoon beef seasoning	15 mL
2 (4 ounce) cans sliced mushrooms, drained	2 (113 g)
2 pounds round steak	1 kg
1 (8 ounce) carton sour cream	1 (227 g)
Hot buttered noodles	

- Combine both cans of mushroom soup, beef broth, beef seasoning and sliced mushrooms. Place in slow cooker and stir to blend.

- Add slices of beef and stir well.

- Cover and cook on LOW for 4 to 5 hours.

- When ready to serve, cook the noodles, drain, add salt and a little butter.

- Stir sour cream into sauce in slow cooker. Spoon sauce and beef over noodles.

Herb-Crusted Beef Roast

1 (2 to 3 pound) beef rump roast	1 (1 to 1.5 kg)
¼ cup chopped fresh parsley	60 mL
¼ cup chopped fresh oregano leaves	60 mL
½ teaspoon dried rosemary leaves	2 mL
1 teaspoon prepared minced garlic	5 mL
1 tablespoon oil	15 mL
6 slices thick-cut bacon	6

- Rub roast with salt and pepper.

- In small bowl, combine parsley, oregano, rosemary, garlic and oil and press mixture on top and sides of roast.

- Place roast in slow cooker. Place bacon over top of beef and tuck ends under bottom.

- Cover and cook on LOW for 6 to 8 hours.

Cola Roast

1 (4 pound) chuck roast	1 (2 kg)
1 (12 ounce) bottle chili sauce	1 (340 g)
1 onion, chopped	1
1 (12 ounce) can cola	1 (340 g)
1 tablespoon worcestershire sauce	15 mL

- Score roast in several places and fill each slit with salt and pepper.

- In skillet, sear roast on all sides. Place in 5-quart (5 L) slow cooker.

- Combine chili sauce, chopped onion, cola and worcestershire and mix well. Pour over roast.

- Cover and cook on LOW for 8 to 9 hours.

Classic Beef Roast

1 (3 to 4 pound) beef chuck roast	1 (1.5 to 2 g)
1 (1.3 ounces) envelope dry onion soup mix	1 (32 g)
2 (10 ounce) cans golden onion soup	2 (284 g)
3 to 4 medium potatoes, quartered	3 to 4

- Place roast in large, slow cooker sprayed with vegetable cooking spray.

- Sprinkle onion soup mix on roast and spoon on undiluted soups. Place potatoes around roast.

- Cover and cook on LOW for 7 to 8 hours or on HIGH for 4 hours.

Mushroom Beef

1 (10 ounce) can beefy mushroom soup	1 (284 g)
1 (10 ounce) can golden mushroom soup	1 (284 g)
1 (10 ounce) can French onion soup	1 (284 g)
½ teaspoon pepper	2 mL
⅓ cup seasoned breadcrumbs	75 mL
2½ pounds premium lean beef stew meat	1.25 kg
Hot buttered noodles	

- In 6-quart (6 L) slow cooker combine soups, pepper, breadcrumbs and ¾ cup (175 mL) water. Stir in beef cubes and mix well.

- Cover and cook on LOW for 8 to 9 hours.

- Serve over hot buttered noodles.

Sweet and Savory Brisket

1 (3 to 4 pound) trimmed beef brisket, halved	1(1.5to2kg)
⅓ cup grape or plum jelly	75 mL
1 cup ketchup	250 mL
1 (1.3 ounces) envelope onion soup mix	1 (32 g)
¾ teaspoon black pepper	4 mL

- Place half of brisket in slow cooker.

- In saucepan, combine jelly, ketchup, onion soup mix and black pepper and heat just enough to mix well.

- Spread half over brisket.

- Top with remaining brisket and jelly-soup mixture.

- Cover and cook on LOW for 8 to 9 hours.

- Slice brisket and serve with cooking juices.

Beef Roast

1 (4 pound) boneless rump roast	1 (2 kg)
½ cup flour, divided	125 mL
1 (1.3 ounce) envelope brown gravy mix	1 (32 g)
1 (1.3 ounce) envelope beefy onion soup mix	1 (32 g)

- Spray 5 to 6-quart (6 L) slow cooker with vegetable cooking spray and cut roast in half (if needed to fit into cooker).

- Place roast in cooker and rub half of flour over roast.

- In small bowl, combine remaining flour, gravy mix and soup mix, gradually add 2 cups (500 mL) water and stir until mixes well. Pour over roast.

- Cover and cook on LOW for 7 to 8 hours or until roast is tender.

Tip: This is a great gravy to serve over mashed potatoes (use instant).

Smoked Brisket

1 (4 to 6 pound) trimmed brisket	1 (2 to 3 kg)
1 (4 ounce) bottle liquid smoke	1 (113 g)
Garlic salt	
Celery salt	
Worcestershire sauce	
1 onion, chopped	1
1 (6 ounce) bottle barbecue sauce	1 (170 g)

- Place brisket in large shallow dish and pour liquid smoke over brisket.

- Sprinkle with garlic salt and celery salt. Cover and chill overnight.

- Before cooking, drain liquid smoke and douse brisket with worcestershire.

- Place chopped onion in slow cooker and place brisket on top of onion.

- Cover and cook on LOW for 7 to 9 hours.

- With 1 hour left on cooking time, pour barbecue sauce over brisket and cook 1 hour.

Good Brisket

½ cup packed brown sugar	125 mL
1 tablespoon Cajun seasoning	15 mL
2 teaspoons lemon pepper	10 mL
1 tablespoon worcestershire sauce	15 mL
1 (3 to 4 pound) trimmed beef brisket	1 (1.5 to 2 kg)

- In small bowl, combine sugar, seasoning, lemon pepper and worcestershire and spread on brisket.

- Place brisket in oblong slow cooker.

- Cover and cook on LOW for 6 to 8 hours.

Easy Brisket

1 (4 to 5 pound) trimmed brisket	1 (2 to 2.5 kg)
1 (1.3 ounces) envelope dry onion soup mix	1 (32 g)
1 (12 ounce) can cola	1 (340 g)
1 (10 ounce) bottle Heinz 57 sauce	1 (284 g)

- Place brisket, fat side up, in slow cooker.

- In bowl, combine onion soup mix, cola and 57 sauce and stir well to remove lumps in soup mix. Pour over brisket.

- Cover and cook on LOW for 8 to 10 hours.

- When ready to serve, let brisket sit at room temperature for about 15 minutes. To serve, cut thin slices across grain of brisket.

Brisket and Gravy

1 (3 to 4 pound) trimmed beef brisket	1 (1.5 to 2 kg)
¼ cup chili sauce	60 mL
1 (1.3 ounce) envelope herb with garlic soup mix	1 (32 g)
2 tablespoons worcestershire sauce	30 mL
3 tablespoons cornstarch	45 mL

- Place beef brisket in 5 to 6-quart (6 L) slow cooker. Cut to fit if necessary.

- In bowl, combine chili sauce, soup mix, worcestershire and 1½ cups (375 mL) water and pour over brisket.

- Cover and cook on LOW for 9 to 11 hours.

- Remove brisket and keep warm. Pour juices into glass measuring cup and skim fat.

- In saucepan stir cornstarch and ¼ cup (60 mL) water. Add 1½ cups (375 mL) cooking liquid and cook, while stirring constantly, until gravy thickens.

- Slice beef thinly across grain and serve with mashed potatoes and gravy.

Shredded Brisket for Sandwiches

2 teaspoons onion powder	10 mL
1 teaspoon minced garlic	5 mL
1 (3 to 4 pound) beef brisket	1 (1.5 to 2 kg)
1 tablespoon liquid smoke	15 mL
1 (16 ounce) bottle barbecue sauce	1 (454 g)

- Combine onion powder, minced garlic and liquid smoke and rub over brisket.

- Place brisket in large slow cooker sprayed with vegetable cooking spray. Add ⅓ cup (75 mL) water to cooker.

- Cover and cook on LOW for 6 to 8 hours or until brisket is tender.

- Remove brisket, cool and reserve ½ cup (125 mL) cooking juices.

- Shred brisket with 2 forks and place in large saucepan. Add ½ cup (125 mL) cooking juices and barbecue sauce and heat thoroughly.

- Make sandwiches with kaiser rolls or hamburger buns.

A Different Corned Beef

2 onions, sliced	2
Lemon pepper	
1 (3 to 4 pound) seasoned corned beef	1 (1.5 to 2 kg)

Glaze:	
¼ cup honey	60 ml
¼ cup frozen orange juice concentrate, thawed	60 mL
1 tablespoon prepared mustard	15 mL

- Place sliced onion in large slow cooker. Add 1 cup (250 mL) water.

- Sprinkle lemon pepper liberally over corned beef and place on top on onion.

- Cover and cook on LOW for 7 to 9 hours.

- Remove corned beef from slow cooker and place in ovenproof pan.

- Preheat oven to 375° (190° C).

- Prepare glaze by combining all ingredients and spoon over corned beef.

- Bake for 30 minutes and baste occasionally with glaze.

Beef Ribs and Gravy

4 to 4½ pounds beef short ribs	**2 to 2.5 kg**
1 onion, sliced	**1**
1 teaspoon seasoned black pepper	**5 mL**
1 (12 ounce) jar beef gravy	**1 (340 g)**
1 (1.3 ounce) envelope beef gravy mix	**1 (32 g)**

- Spray 6-quart (6 L) slow cooker with vegetable cooking spray and place beef ribs inside.

- Cover with onion and sprinkle with black pepper.

- In small bowl, combine beef gravy and dry gravy mix and pour over ribs and onion.

- Cover and cook on LOW for 9 to 11 hours.
  (The ribs must cook this long on LOW to tenderize.)

- Serve with hot mashed potatoes and gravy.

Beef and Noodles al Grande

1½ pounds lean ground beef	750 g
1 (16 ounce) package frozen onions and bell peppers, thawed	1 (450 g)
1 (16 ounce) box processed cheese, cubed	1 (450 g)
2 (15 ounce) cans Mexican stewed tomatoes, liquid reserved	1 (420 g)
2 (15 ounce) cans whole kernel corn, drained	2 (420 g)
1 (8 ounce) package medium egg noodles	1 (225 g)
1 cup shredded cheddar cheese	250 mL

- In skillet, brown ground beef and drain fat.

- Place beef in 5 to 6-quart (6 L) slow cooker, add onion, peppers, cheese, tomatoes, corn and about 1 teaspoon (5 mL) salt and mix well.

- Cover and cook on LOW for 4 to 5 hours.

- Cook noodles according to package direction, drain and fold into beef-tomato mixture.

- Cook another 30 minutes to heat thoroughly.

- When ready to serve, top with cheddar cheese, several sprinkles of chopped fresh parsley or chopped fresh green onions.

Stuffed Cabbage

10 to 12 large cabbage leaves	10 to 12
1¼ pounds lean ground beef	650 kg
½ cup brown rice	125 mL
1 egg, beaten	1
1 teaspoon seasoned salt	5 mL
½ teaspoon seasoned pepper	2 mL
¼ teaspoon ground cinnamon	1 mL
1 (15 ounce) can tomato sauce	1 (438 g)

- Wash cabbage leaves, place in saucepan of boiling water and turn off heat. Soak about 5 minutes. (If you can't get 10 to 12 large leaves, put two together to make one large leaf.)

- Remove leaves, drain and cool.

- In bowl, combine beef, rice, egg, seasoned salt, pepper, cinnamon and mix well.

- Place about 2 tablespoons (30 mL) beef mixture on each cabbage leaf and roll tightly.

- Stack rolls in oblong slow cooker sprayed with vegetable cooking spray. Pour tomato sauce over rolls.

- Cover and cook on HIGH for 1 hour; lower heat to LOW and cook another 6 to 7 hours.

Southwest Spaghetti

1½ pounds lean ground beef	750 kg
2½ teaspoons chili powder	12 mL
1 (15 ounce) can tomato sauce	1 (438 g)
1 (7 ounce) package spaghetti, uncooked	1 (210 g)
1 heaping tablespoon beef seasoning	15 mL
Shredded cheddar-jack cheese	

- In skillet, brown ground beef until no longer pink. Place in 4 to 5-quart (5 L) slow cooker.

- Add chili powder, tomato sauce, spaghetti, 2⅓ cups (575 mL) water and beef seasoning and mix well.

- Cover and cook on LOW for 6 to 7 hours.

- When ready to serve, cover with lots of shredded cheddar-jack cheese.

Beef and Gravy

2 pounds sirloin steak or thick round steak	1 kg
Oil	
1 (1.3 ounces) envelope dry onion soup mix	1 (32 g)
1 (10 ounce) can golden mushroom soup	1 (284 g)
1 (4 ounce) can sliced mushrooms	1 (113 g)
Hot buttered noodles	

- Cut steak in ½-inch pieces.

- Brown beef in skillet in a little oil and place in 5 to 6-quart (6 L) slow cooker.

- Combine onion soup mix, mushroom soup, mushrooms and ½ cup (125 mL) water. Spoon over top of beef and mix well.

- Cover and cook on LOW for 7 to 8 hours.

- Serve over hot cooked noodles.

Sauce for Fancy Meatballs

1 (16 ounce) can whole-berry cranberry sauce	1 (454 g)
1 cup ketchup	250 mL
⅔ cup packed brown sugar	150 mL
½ cup beef broth	125 mL
1 (28 ounce) package prepared meatballs, thawed	1 (800 g)

- Combine cranberry sauce, ketchup, brown sugar and beef broth in large slow cooker.

- Turn heat to HIGH and let mixture come to boil, about 30 minutes to 1 hour. Place package of thawed meatballs in with sauce.

- Cover and cook on LOW for 2 hours.

- Remove meatballs to serving dish with slotted spoon and serve with toothpicks as appetizers or for supper or buffet pick-up food.

Meat and Potatoes

4 medium potatoes, peeled, sliced	4
1¼ pounds lean ground beef, browned	650 kg
1 onion, sliced	1
1 (10 ounce) can cream of mushroom soup	1 (284 g)
1 (10 ounce) can vegetable beef soup	1 (284 g)
Salt and pepper to taste	

- In large slow cooker, layer all ingredients.

- Cover and cook on LOW for 5 to 6 hours.

Make-Believe Lasagna

1 pound lean ground beef	500 g
1 onion, chopped	1
½ teaspoon garlic powder	2 mL
1 (18 ounce) can spaghetti sauce	1 (510 g)
½ teaspoon ground oregano	2 mL
6 to 8 lasagna noodles, uncooked, divided	6 to 8
1 (12 ounce) carton cottage cheese, divided	1 (340 g)
½ cup parmesan cheese, divided	125 mL
1 (12 ounce) package shredded mozzarella cheese, divided	1 (340 g)

- Brown ground beef and onion in large skillet. Add garlic powder, spaghetti sauce and oregano. Cook just until thoroughly warmed.

- Spoon layer of meat sauce onto bottom of greased oblong slow cooker. Add layer of uncooked lasagna noodles (break to fit slow cooker).

- Top with layer of half remaining meat sauce, half cottage cheese, half parmesan cheese and half mozzarella cheese. Repeat layering and start with more lasagna noodles.

- Cover and cook on LOW for 6 to 8 hours.

Mac 'N Cheese Supper

1½ pounds lean ground beef	750 g
1 teaspoon seasoned salt	5 mL
2 (7 ounce) packages macaroni and cheese dinners	2 (200 g)
1 (15 ounce) can whole kernel corn, drained	1 (438 g)
1½ cups shredded Monterey Jack cheese	375 mL

- In large skillet, sprinkle ground beef with seasoned salt, brown until no longer pink and drain.

- Prepare macaroni and cheese according to package directions.

- Spray 5-quart (5 L) slow cooker with vegetable cooking spray. Spoon in beef, macaroni and corn and mix well.

- Cover and cook on LOW for 4 to 5 hours.

- When ready to serve, sprinkle cheese over top and leave in cooker until cheese melts.

Meat on the Table

1½ to 2 pounds lean ground beef	750 g to 1 kg
1 (1.3 ounce) envelope beefy onion soup mix	1 (32 g)
⅔ cup quick oats	150 mL
2 eggs	2
1 (12 ounce) bottle chili sauce, divided	1 (340 g)
1 teaspoon black pepper	5 mL

- Make foil handles for slow cooker. (See page 192.) Spray 5 to 6-quart (6 L) oval slow cooker with vegetable cooking spray.

- In bowl, combine beef, onion soup mix, oats, eggs, ¾ cup (175 mL) chili sauce and black pepper and mix well.

- With your hands, shape meat mixture into round ball, place in slow cooker and pat down into loaf shape.

- Cover and cook on LOW for 3 to 4 hours.

- Before last half hour of cooking time, spread remaining chili sauce over top of loaf and continue cooking. Use foil handles to lift meat loaf out of slow cooker.

Jack's Meat Loaf

2 pounds lean ground beef	1 kg
2 eggs	2
½ cup chili sauce	125 mL
1¼ cups seasoned breadcrumbs	300 mL
1 (8 ounce) package shredded Monterey Jack cheese, divided	1 (225 g)

- Spray 5-quart (5 L) oblong slow cooker with vegetable cooking spray.

- Make foil handles in slow cooker. (See page 192.)

- Combine beef, eggs, chili sauce and breadcrumbs and mix well.

- With your hands, shape half of beef mixture into flat loaf and place in bottom of slow cooker sprayed with vegetable cooking spray.

- Sprinkle half cheese over meat loaf and press into meat.

- Form remaining meat mixture in same shape as first layer and place over cheese.

- Cover and cook on LOW for 6 to 7 hours.

- When ready to serve, sprinkle remaining cheese over loaf and leave in cooker until cheese melts.

- Carefully remove loaf with foil handles and place on serving plate.

Hash Brown Dinner

1½ pounds lean ground chuck, browned	750 g
1 (1.3 ounce) envelope brown gravy	1 (32 g)
1 (15 ounce) can cream corn	1 (438 g)
1 (15 ounce) can whole kernel corn	1 (438 g)
1 (8 ounce) package shredded cheddar cheese, divided	1 (225 g)
1 (16 ounce) package frozen hash browns, partially thawed	1 (454 g)
1 (10 ounce) can golden mushroom soup	1 (284 g)
1 (5 ounce) can evaporated milk	1 (140 g)

- Place browned beef in slow cooker and toss with dry brown gravy.

- Add cream corn and whole kernel corn and cover with half cheddar cheese.

- Top with hash browns and remaining cheese.

- In bowl, combine mushroom soup and evaporated milk. Mix well and pour over hash browns and cheese.

- Cover and cook on LOW for 6 to 8 hours.

Slow Cooker

Fiesta Beef and Rice

1½ pounds lean ground beef	750 g
1 (15 ounce) can Mexican stewed tomatoes	1 (438 g)
1 (6.8 ounce) box beef-flavored rice mix	1 (190 g)
1 (15 ounce) can Mexican corn, drained	1 (438 g)
Salsa	

- Spray 5-quart (5 L) oblong slow cooker with vegetable cooking spray.

- Sprinkle salt and pepper over ground beef and shape into small patties.

- Place in bottom of slow cooker.

- In separate bowl, combine stewed tomatoes, rice mix, corn and 2 cups (500 mL) water and mix well. Spoon over beef patties.

- Cover and cook on LOW for 4 to 5 hours.

- When ready to serve, place large spoonful of salsa on each serving.

Cowboy Feed

1½ pounds lean ground beef	750 g
2 onions, coarsely chopped	2
5 medium potatoes, peeled, sliced	5
1 (15 ounce) can kidney beans, rinsed, drained	1 (438 g)
1 (15 ounce) can pinto beans, drained	1 (438 g)
1 (15 ounce) can Mexican stewed tomatoes	1 (438 g)
1 (10 ounce) can tomato soup	1 (284 g)
½ teaspoon basil	2 mL
½ teaspoon oregano	2 mL
2 teaspoons minced garlic	10 mL

- In skillet, sprinkle beef with some salt and pepper, brown and drain.

- Place onions in bottom of slow cooker and spoon beef over onions.

- On top of beef, layer potatoes and kidney and pinto beans.

- Pour stewed tomatoes and tomato soup over beans and potatoes and sprinkle with basil, oregano and garlic.

- Cover and cook on LOW for 7 to 8 hours.

Cheeseburger Supper

1 (5 ounce) box bacon and cheddar scalloped potatoes	1 (140 g)
2¼ cups boiling water	560 mL
⅓ cup milk	75 mL
4 tablespoons (¼ stick) butter, melted	60 mL
1½ pounds lean ground beef	750g
1 onion, coarsely chopped	1
1 (15 ounce) can whole kernel corn, liquid reserved	1 (438 g)
1 (8 ounce) package shredded cheddar cheese	1 (225 g)

- In slow cooker sprayed with vegetable cooking spray, place scalloped potatoes.

- Pour boiling water, milk and butter over potatoes.

- In skillet, brown ground beef and onion in little oil, drain and spoon over potatoes. Top with corn.

- Cover and cook on LOW for 6 to 7 hours.

- When ready to serve, sprinkle cheese over corn.

Beef and Macaroni Supper

1 (10 ounce) package macaroni, cooked, drained	1 (284 g)
3 tablespoons oil	45 mL
1½ pounds lean ground beef, browned, drained	750 g
1 onion, chopped	1
3 ribs celery, chopped	3
2 (10 ounce) cans tomato soup	2 (284 g)
1 (6 ounce) can tomato paste	1 (170 g)
1 teaspoon beef bouillon	5 mL
1 (8 ounce) package cubed processed cheese	1 (225 g)

- Toss cooked macaroni with oil to make sure macaroni does not stick.

- Place in slow cooker sprayed with vegetable cooking spray.

- Add beef, onion, celery, tomato soup, tomato paste, beef bouillon and ⅔ cup (150 mL) water and stir to mix well.

- Cover and cook on LOW for 4 to 6 hours. Before the last hour of cooking time, stir in cubed cheese.

Beef and Bean Medley

1 pound lean ground beef	500 g
1 onion, chopped	1
6 slices bacon, cooked and crumbled	6
2 (15 ounce) cans pork and beans	2 (420 g)
1 (15 ounce) can butter beans, rinsed, drained	1 (420 g)
1 (15 ounce) can kidney beans, rinsed, drained	1 (420 g)
½ cup ketchup	125 mL
½ cup packed brown sugar	125 mL
3 tablespoons vinegar	45 mL
1 (13 ounce) bag small size corn chips	1 (380 g)
1 (8 ounce) package shredded cheddar cheese	1 (225 g)

- In skillet, brown ground beef and onion, drain and transfer to 4 to 5-quart (5 L) slow cooker.

- Add bacon and all 4 cans beans.

- In bowl, combine ketchup, brown sugar and vinegar. Add to cooker and stir.

- Cover and cook on LOW for 4 to 6 hours.

- When ready to serve, spoon over corn chips and sprinkle cheese over top.

Italian Tortellini

½ pound ground round steak	250 g
1 pound bulk Italian sausage	500 g
1 (15 ounce) carton refrigerated marinara sauce	1 (438 g)
1 (15 ounce) can Italian stewed tomatoes, liquid reserved	1 (438 g)
1½ cups sliced fresh mushrooms	375 mL
1 (9 ounce) package refrigerated cheese tortellini	1 (250 g)
1½ cups shredded mozzarella cheese	375 mL

- Brown and cook ground beef and sausage in large skillet about 10 minutes and drain.

- In 4 to 5-quart (5 L) slow cooker, combine meat mixture, marinara sauce, tomatoes and mushrooms.

- Cover and cook on LOW 6 to 8 hours.

- Stir in tortellini and sprinkle with mozzarella cheese.

- Turn cooker to HIGH and continue cooking for another 10 to 15 minutes or until tortellini is tender.

Sloppy Joes

3 pounds ground beef	2 kg
1 tablespoon minced garlic	15 mL
1 large onion, finely chopped	1
2 ribs celery, chopped	2
¼ cup packed brown sugar	60 mL
3½ tablespoons prepared mustard	52 mL
1 tablespoon chili powder	15 mL
1½ cups ketchup	375 mL
3 tablespoons worcestershire sauce	45 mL

- Brown beef, garlic and onion in very large skillet and drain.

- Combine celery, brown sugar, mustard, chili powder, ketchup and worcestershire in sprayed 5-quart (5 L) slow cooker. Stir in meat mixture.

- Cover and cook on LOW heat for 6 to 7 hours.

  Tip: This will make enough to fill 16 to 18 hamburger buns.

Special Hot Dog Supper

1 pound beef wieners	500 g
2 (15 ounce) cans chili without beans	2 (438 g)
1 onion, finely chopped	1
1 (10 ounce) can cheddar cheese soup	1 (284 g)
1 (10 ounce) can fiesta nacho cheese soup	1 (284 g)
1 (7 ounce) can chopped green chilies, drained	1 (193 g)

- Cut wieners in ½-inch pieces and place in slow cooker.

- In saucepan, combine chili, onion, cheese soup, nacho cheese soup and green chilies. (Omit green chilies if serving to kids.)

- Heat just enough to mix ingredients well. Spoon over wieners.

- Cover and cook on LOW for 1½ hours to 2½ hours.

- Serve over bowl of small corn chips or crisp tortilla chips slightly crushed.

PORK

Stuffed Pork Chops

4 or 5 (1-inch) pork chops	4 or 5
1 (15 ounce) can mixed vegetables, well drained	1 (438 g)
1 (8 ounce) can whole kernel corn, drained	1 (225 g)
½ cup uncooked rice	125 mL
1 cup Italian-style seasoned, dry breadcrumbs	250 mL
1 (15 ounce) can stewed tomatoes, slightly drained	1 (438 g)

- Cut pocket in each pork chop and season with salt and pepper.

- In large bowl combine mixed vegetables, corn, rice and breadcrumbs and stuff pork chops with vegetable mixture. Secure open sides with toothpicks.

- Place any remaining vegetable mixture in bottom of 5-quart (5 L) slow cooker. Add pork chops and spoon stewed tomatoes over top of pork chops.

- Cover and cook on LOW for 8 to 9 hours.

- Serve vegetable mixture along with pork chops.

Smothered Pork Chop Dinner

6 (¾ inch) bone-in pork chops	6
8 to 10 medium red (new) potatoes, unpeeled	8 to 10
2 onions, sliced	2
1 (10 ounce) can cream of chicken soup	1 (284 g)
½ cup chicken broth	125 mL
¼ cup Dijon mustard	60 mL
1 teaspoon dried basil leaves	5 mL

- In non-stick skillet, brown pork chops sprinkled with salt and pepper.

- Place potatoes and onions in bottom of 5 or 6-quart (6 L) slow cooker and add browned pork chops.

- In saucepan, combine chicken soup, broth, mustard and basil and heat just enough to mix well. Pour over pork chops.

- Cover and cook on LOW for 7 to 9 hours.

Tip: To "dress" these pork chops up, sprinkle with 1 (3 ounce) (85 g) can fried onion rings.

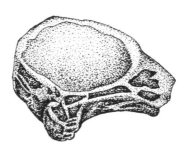

Savory Pork Chops

6 (¾-inch) pork chops	6
1 cup pineapple juice	250 mL
⅓ cup packed brown sugar	75 mL
3 tablespoons cider vinegar	45 mL

- In skillet, brown pork chops on both sides and place in 5-quart (5 L) slow cooker.

- Combine pineapple juice, brown sugar and vinegar and mix well.

- Pour brown sugar-vinegar mixture over pork chops.

- Cover and cook on LOW for 4 to 5 hours.

- Serve over hot cooked noodles.

Ranch Pork Chops

6 (¾-inch) bone-in pork chops	6
1 (1.3 ounce) packet ranch dressing mix	1 (32 g)
½ teaspoon black pepper	2 mL
2 (15 ounce) cans new potatoes, drained, quartered	2 (438 g)
1 (10 ounce) can French onion soup	1 (284 g)

- Spray 6-quart (6 L) oblong slow cooker with vegetable cooking spray. Place pork chops on bottom of slow cooker.

- Sprinkle pork chops with ranch dressing mix and black pepper.

- Place potatoes around pork chops and pour French onion soup around potatoes and chops.

- Cover and cook on LOW for 4 to 5 hours.

Pork Chops with Orange Sauce

2 medium sliced yellow squash	2
2 onions, sliced	2
6 to 8 bone-in pork chops	6 to 8
½ cup chicken broth	125 mL
½ cup orange marmalade	125 mL
1 tablespoon honey mustard	15 mL
2 tablespoons cornstarch	30 mL

- Place squash and onions in bottom of 5 to-6 quart (6 L) slow cooker.

- Sprinkle salt and pepper on pork chops and place on top of vegetables.

- In bowl combine broth, marmalade and mustard and spoon over pork chops.

- Cover and cook on LOW for 4 to 6 hours.

- Transfer pork chops and vegetables to serving plate and cover to keep warm.

- For sauce, pour liquid from slow cooker into medium saucepan. Combine about 2 tablespoons (30 mL) water with cornstarch and add to saucepan.

- Heat while stirring constantly until mixture thickens. Serve chops and vegetables with sauce.

Pork Chops for Supper

6 (¾-inch thick) pork loin chops	6
1 onion, halved, sliced	1
1 (8 ounce) can tomato sauce	1 (225 g)
¼ cup packed brown sugar	60 mL
1 tablespoon worcestershire sauce	15 mL
1 teaspoon seasoned salt	5 mL

- In skillet, brown pork chops on both sides and place in 4 to 5-quart (5 L) slow cooker. Place onions over pork chops.

- Combine tomato sauce, brown sugar, worcestershire sauce, seasoned salt and ¼ cup (60 mL) water and spoon over onions and pork chops.

- Cover and cook on LOW for 4 to 5 hours.

Pork Chops and Gravy

6 (½-inch) thick pork chops	6
8 to 10 new potatoes, unpeeled, quartered	8 to 10
1 (16 ounce) package baby carrots	1 (454 g)
2 (10 ounce) cans cream of mushroom soup with roasted garlic	1 (284 g)

- Sprinkle salt and pepper on pork chops.

- In skillet, brown pork chops and place in 5 to 6-quart (6 L) slow cooker. Place potatoes and carrots around pork chops.

- In saucepan, heat mushroom soup with ½ cup (125 mL) water and pour over chops and vegetables.

- Cover and cook on LOW for 6 to 7 hours.

Pork Chops Pizza

6 (1-inch) thick boneless pork chops	6
Salt and pepper	
Oil	
1 onion, finely chopped	1
1 green bell pepper, finely chopped	1
1 (8 ounce) jar pizza sauce	1 (227 g)
1 (10 ounce) box plain couscous	1 (284 g)
2 tablespoons (¼ stick) butter	30 mL
1 cup shredded mozzarella cheese	250 mL

- Trim fat from pork chops and sprinkle with salt and pepper.

- In skillet, brown and cook pork chops on both sides about 5 minutes.

- Transfer chops to oblong slow cooker sprayed with vegetable cooking spray.

- Spoon onion and bell pepper over chops and pour pizza sauce over top.

- Cover and cook on LOW for 4 to 6 hours.

- Cook couscous according to package directions adding 2 tablespoons (¼ stick) (30 mL) butter instead of 1 tablespoon (15 mL) suggested and place on serving platter.

- Spoon chops and sauce over couscous and sprinkle cheese over chops.

Pineapple-Pork Chops

6 to 8 (½-inch) thick boneless pork chops	6 to 8
1 (6 ounce) can frozen pineapple juice concentrate, thawed	1 (170 g)
¼ cup packed brown sugar	60 mL
⅓ cup wine or tarragon vinegar	75 mL
⅓ cup honey	75 mL
1 (6.2 ounce) package parmesan and butter rice	1 (170 g)

- In skillet, brown pork chops in a little oil and transfer to slow cooker sprayed with vegetable cooking spray.

- In bowl, combine pineapple juice, sugar, vinegar and honey. Pour over pork chops.

- Cover and cook on LOW for 5 to 6 hours.

- Serve over hot buttered rice.

Delicious Pork Chops

1¾ cups flour	430 mL
Scant 2 tablespoons dry mustard	30 mL
8 boneless, thick pork chops	8
Oil	
1 (10 ounce) can condensed chicken and rice soup	1 (284 g)

- Place flour and mustard in shallow bowl. Dredge pork chops in flour-mustard mixture.

- In skillet, brown pork chops in a little oil. Place all chops in oblong 6-quart (6 L) slow cooker.

- Pour soup over chicken and add about ¼ cup (50 mL) water.

- Cover and cook on LOW for 6 to 8 hours.

Peachy Pork Chops

6 to 8 (¾ inch) thick bone-in pork chops	**6 to 8**
½ cup packed brown sugar	**125 mL**
¼ teaspoon ground cinnamon	**1 mL**
¼ teaspoon ground cloves	**1 mL**
1 (8 ounce) can tomato sauce	**1 (225 g)**
1 (29 ounce) can peach halves, liquid reserved	**1 (800 g)**
¼ cup white vinegar	**60 mL**

- In skillet, brown pork chops on both sides and place in oblong slow cooker.

- Combine sugar, cinnamon, cloves, tomato sauce, ¼ cup (60 mL) syrup from peaches and vinegar.

- Pour sugar-tomato sauce mixture over pork chops and place peach halves over top.

- Cover and cook on LOW for 4 to 5 hours.

Italian Pork Chops

6 to 8 (1-inch) thick boneless pork chops	6 to 8
½ pound fresh mushrooms, sliced	250 g
1 (10 ounce) package frozen seasoning blend onions and bell peppers, thawed	1 (284 g)
1 teaspoon Italian seasoning	5 mL
1 (15 ounce) can Italian stewed tomatoes	1 (438 g)

- In skillet, brown pork chops, sprinkled with salt and pepper on both sides.

- In 6-quart (6 L) slow cooker, combine mushrooms, seasoning blend and Italian seasoning.

- Place pork chops over vegetables and pour Italian stewed tomatoes over pork chops.

- Cover and cook on LOW for 7 to 8 hours.

- To serve, spoon mushroom-seasoning blend over pork chops.

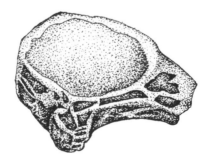

Honey-Mustard Pork Chops
Try this sauce over hot, cooked rice. It is wonderful!

1 (10 ounce) can golden mushroom soup	1 (284 g)
⅓ cup white wine	75 mL
¼ cup honey mustard	60 mL
1 teaspoon minced garlic	5 mL
1 teaspoon salt	5 mL
4 to 5 (¾-inch) thick pork chops	4 to 5

- In large bowl, combine soup, wine, honey mustard, minced garlic and salt and mix well.

- Place pork chops, sprinkled with a little black pepper, in 5-quart (5 L) slow cooker and spoon soup-honey-mustard mixture over chops.

- Cover and cook on LOW for 5 to 6 hours.

- When ready to serve, lift pork chops out of sauce and onto serving plate. Stir sauce to mix well and serve over pork chops.

Tip: For a "meat and potato meal", just slice 3 potatoes and place in slow cooker before adding pork chops.

"Baked" Pork Chops

6 to 8 medium thick pork chops	6 to 8
1 (10 ounce) can cream of chicken soup	1 (284 g)
3 tablespoons ketchup	45 mL
1 tablespoon worcestershire sauce	15 mL
1 onion, chopped	1

- In skillet, brown pork chops in a little oil and season with salt and pepper.

- Place pork chops in slow cooker.

- In bowl, combine chicken soup, ketchup, worcestershire and onion and pour over pork chops.

- Cover and cook on LOW for 5 to 6 hours.

Tender Pork Loin

1 (3 to 4 pound) pork loin	1 (1.5 to 2 kg)
2 teaspoons minced garlic	10 mL
½ teaspoon rosemary	2 mL
1 teaspoon sage	5 mL
1½ teaspoons marjoram	7 mL

- Place pork loin in slow cooker, rub with minced garlic and sprinkle with rosemary, sage and marjoram. Add about ¼ cup (60 mL) water to bottom of slow cooker.

- Cover and cook on LOW heat for 4 to 5 hours.

Tip: Sometimes it is hard to buy a small (3 to 4 pound) (1.5 to 2 kg) pork loin, but they are always available in long (8 or 9-pound) (4 to 4.5 kg) pork loins. Because pork loin is such a good cut (no bones – no fat), think about buying the whole loin, cut it into 2 or 3 pieces and freeze two pieces.

Pork Roast with Apricot Glaze

1 (3 pound) boneless pork roast	1 (1.5 kg)
⅓ cup chicken broth	50 mL
1 (18 ounce) jar apricot preserves	1 (510 g)
2 tablespoons dijon mustard	30 mL
1 onion, finely chopped	1
1 green bell pepper, finely chopped	1

- Trim fat from roast and, if necessary, cut roast to fit into sprayed 4 to 5-quart (5 L) slow cooker. Place roast in cooker.

- In saucepan combine broth, preserves, mustard, onion and bell pepper and heat just enough to mix ingredients well and pour over roast.

- Cover and cook on LOW for 9 to 11 hours or on HIGH for 5 to 6 hours.

- Transfer meat to serving plate.

- Sauce left in cooker is delicious as is or thickened. To thicken sauce, mix 1 tablespoon (15 mL) cornstarch and 2 tablespoons (30 mL) water. Place in saucepan and add sauce from cooker.

- Heat, stirring constantly, until sauce thickens slightly.

- Sauce may be served with hot cooked rice or just spooned over roast.

Fruit-Stuffed Pork Roast

1 (3 to 3½ pound) boneless loin pork roast	1 (1.5 to 2 kg)
1 cup mixed dried fruits	250 mL
1 tablespoon dried onion flakes	15 mL
1 teaspoon salt	5 mL
1 teaspoon thyme leaves	5 mL
½ teaspoon ground cinnamon	2 mL
½ teaspoon black pepper	2 mL
2 tablespoons oil	30 mL
½ cup apple cider	125 mL

- Place pork on cutting board. Cut horizontally through center of pork almost to opposite side. Open pork like a book.

- Layer dried fruits and onion in opening. Bring halves of pork together and tie at 1-inch intervals with kitchen twine.

- In small bowl, combine salt, thyme, cinnamon and black pepper and rub into roast.

- Place roast in skillet with oil and brown roast on all sides.

- Place roast in slow cooker sprayed with vegetable cooking spray and pour apple cider in bottom of cooker.

- Cover and cook on LOW for 3 to 4 hours. Partially cool before slicing.

Country Pork Chops

7 to 8 new potatoes, unpeeled, sliced	7 to 8
2 onions, sliced	2
1 (10 ounce) can cream of celery soup	1 (284 g)
⅓ cup chicken broth	75 mL
3 tablespoons dijon mustard	45 mL
1 (4 ounce) can sliced mushrooms, drained	1 (125 g)
1 teaspoon minced garlic	5 mL
¾ teaspoon dried basil	4 mL
8 boneless pork chops	8

- Place potatoes and onions in large slow cooker.

- In bowl, combine soup, broth, mustard, mushrooms, garlic and basil, mix well and pour over potatoes and onions. Stir to coat vegetables.

- Sprinkle pork chops with a little salt and pepper. In skillet brown both sides of pork chops in a little oil.

- Place chops over vegetables.

- Cover and cook on LOW for 6 to 7 hours.

Spinach-Stuffed Pork Roast

1 (2 to 2½ pounds) pork tenderloin	1 (1 to 1.5 kg)
1 (10 ounce) package frozen chopped spinach, thawed	1 (284 g)
1 teaspoon minced garlic	5 mL
⅓ cup seasoned breadcrumbs	75 mL
⅓ cup grated parmesan cheese	75 mL
2 tablespoons oil	30 mL
½ teaspoon seasoned salt	2 mL

- To prepare tenderloin for stuffing, cut horizontally down length about ½-inch from top to within ¾-inch of opposite end and open flat.

- Turn pork so you can cut other side, from inside edge to outer edge and open flat. If one side is thicker than other side, cover with plastic wrap and pound until both sides are ¾-inch thick.

- Squeeze spinach with several sheets of paper towels several times until all liquid is gone.

- Combine spinach, garlic, breadcrumbs and cheese and mix well.

- Spread mixture on inside surfaces of pork and press down. Roll up pork and tie with kitchen twine.

- Heat oil in large skillet over medium to high heat and brown pork on all sides.

- Place pork in oblong slow cooker and sprinkle with salt.

- Cover and cook on LOW for 6 to 8 hours.

Pork and Cabbage Supper

1 (16 ounce) package baby carrots	1 (454 g)
1 cup chicken broth	250 mL
1 (1.3 ounce) package golden onion soup mix	1 (32 g)
1 (3 to 4 pound) pork shoulder roast	1 (1.5 to 2 kg)
1 medium head cabbage	1

- Place carrots in 5-quart (5 L) slow cooker.

- Add chicken broth and 1 cup (250 mL) water. Sprinkle dry soup mix and lots of black pepper over carrots.

- Cut roast in half (if needed to fit in cooker) and place over carrot mixture.

- Cover and cook on LOW for 6 to 7 hours.

- Cut cabbage in small-size chunks and place over roast. Cover and cook another 1 to 2 hours or until cabbage cooks.

Home-Style Ribs

4 to 6 pounds boneless pork spareribs	2 to 2.5 kg
1 cup chili sauce	250 mL
1 cup packed brown sugar	250 mL
2 tablespoons vinegar	30 mL
2 tablespoons worcestershire sauce	30 mL

- Sprinkle ribs liberally with salt and pepper. Place ribs in slow cooker.

- Combine ½ cup water, chili sauce, brown sugar, vinegar and worcestershire and spoon over ribs.

- Cover and cook on LOW for 5 to 6 hours.

Roasted Red Pepper Tenderloin

2 pounds pork tenderloins	1 kg
1 (1.3 ounce) packet ranch dressing mix	1 (32 g)
1 cup roasted red bell peppers, rinsed, chopped	250 mL
1 (8 ounce) carton sour cream	1 (225 g)

- In large skillet, brown both tenderloins and place in 6-quart (6 L) oblong slow cooker.

- Combine ranch dressing mix, red bell peppers and ½ cup (125 mL) water and spoon over pork tenderloins.

- Cover and cook on LOW for 4 to 5 hours.

- When ready to serve, remove tenderloins from slow cooker.

- Stir sour cream into sauce made. Serve over tenderloin slices.

Walnut Ham

½ pound cooked ham slices	250 g
2 (10 ounce) cans cream of onion soup	2 (284 g)
⅓ cup grated parmesan cheese	75 mL
⅔ cup chopped walnuts	150 mL
Hot, cooked linguine	

- Cut ham into ½-inch strips.

- Place soups, cheese, walnuts and ham strips in slow cooker.

- Cover and cook on LOW for 1 to 2 hours or until hot and bubbly.

- Serve over hot, cooked linguine.

Honey-Mustard Pork Roast

1 green bell pepper, chopped	1
1 sweet red bell pepper, chopped	1
2 yellow onions, chopped	2
3 tablespoons sweet and tangy honey mustard	45 mL
1 (2 to 2½ pound) pork loin roast	1 (1 to 1.5 kg)

- Combine bell peppers and onions in 4 to 6-quart slow cooker.

- Rub honey mustard liberally over pork loin with most of honey mustard on top of roast.

- Cook on LOW for 4 to 6 hours. Place roast on serving platter.

- Spoon bell peppers, onions and pan juices in small serving bowl and spoon over slices of roast to serve.

Delectable Apricot Ribs

4 to 5 pounds baby back pork loin ribs	2 to 2.5 kg
1 (16 ounce) jar apricot preserves	1 (454 g)
⅓ cup soy sauce	75 mL
¼ cup packed light brown sugar	60 mL
2 teaspoons garlic powder	10 mL

- Spray large slow cooker with vegetable cooking spray and place ribs in cooker.

- In bowl, combine preserves, soy sauce, brown sugar and garlic powder and spoon over ribs.

- Cover and cook on LOW for 6 to 7 hours.

Ginger Pork

1 (2 to 2½ pounds) boneless pork roast	1 (1 to 1.5 kg)
1 cup chicken broth	250 mL
3½ tablespoons quick-cooking tapioca	52 mL
3 tablespoons soy sauce	5 mL
1 teaspoon grated fresh ginger	5 mL
1 (15 ounce) can pineapple chunks, drain, juice reserved	1 (438 g)
1 (16 ounce) package baby carrots	1 (454 g)
1 (8 ounce) can sliced water chestnuts, drained	1 (225 g)

- Trim fat from pork. Cut pork into 1-inch pieces, brown in large skillet and drain.

- In sprayed 4 to 5-quart (5 L) slow cooker combine chicken broth, tapioca, soy sauce, ginger, pineapple juice, carrots and water chestnuts. (Chill pineapple chunks in refrigerator until ready to include in recipe.)

- Add browned pork.

- Cover and cook on LOW for 6 to 8 hours.

- Turn heat to HIGH and stir in pineapple chunks. Cover and cook for another 10 minutes.

- Serve over hot cooked rice.

Barbecue Pork Roast

Use leftovers for great sandwiches.

1 onion, thinly sliced	**1**
2 tablespoons flour	**30 mL**
1 (2 to 3 pound) pork shoulder roast	**1 (1 to 1.5 kg)**
1 (8 ounce) bottle barbecue sauce	**1 (225 g)**
1 tablespoon chili powder	**15 mL**
1 teaspoon ground cumin	**5 mL**

- Separate onion slices into rings and place in 4 to 5-quart (5 L) slow cooker. Sprinkle flour over onions.

- If necessary, cut roast to fit cooker and place over onions.

- In bowl, combine barbecue sauce, chili powder and cumin and pour over roast.

- Cover and cook on LOW for 10 to 12 hours.

- Remove roast from cooker and slice. Serve sauce over sliced roast.

    Tip: To make sandwiches, shred roast and return to cooker. Cook another 30 minutes to heat thoroughly.

Tangy Apricot Ribs

3 to 4 pounds baby back, pork loin ribs	1.5 to 2 kg
1 (16 ounce) jar apricot preserves	1 (454 g)
⅓ cup soy sauce	75 mL
¼ cup packed light brown sugar	60 mL

- Place ribs in large slow cooker sprayed with vegetable cooking spray.

- In bowl combine preserves, soy sauce and brown sugar and spoon over ribs.

- Cover and cook on LOW for 6 to 8 hours.

Finger Lickin' Baby Backs

2½ to 3 pounds baby back pork ribs	1 to 1.5 kg
Black pepper	
½ cup chili sauce	125 mL
⅓ cup apple cider vinegar	75 mL
½ cup packed brown sugar	125 mL

- Spray sides of 5 to 6-quart (6 L) slow cooker with vegetable cooking spray.

- Cut ribs in serving-size pieces, sprinkle with black pepper and place in slow cooker.

- Combine chili sauce, vinegar, brown sugar and about ¾ cup (175 mL) water and pour over ribs.

- Cover and cook on LOW for about 6 to 7 hours.

- After about 3 hours, you might move ribs around in slow cooker so sauce is spread over all ribs.

Zesty Ham Supper

1 (28 ounce) package frozen hash brown potatoes with onion and peppers, thawed	1 (800 g)
3 cups diced, cooked ham	750 mL
1 (10 ounce) box frozen green peas, thawed	1 (284 g)
2 (10 ounce) cans fiesta nacho cheese soup	2 (284 g)
1 cup milk	250 mL
1 bunch fresh green onions, chopped	1

- Spray 5 to 6-quart (6 L) slow cooker with vegetable cooking spray.

- Place potatoes, ham and peas in slow cooker and stir to mix.

- In bowl, combine soup and milk and mix well. Pour over potato mixture and mix well.

- Cover and cook on LOW for 6 to 8 hours.

- Sprinkle green onions over top when ready to serve.

Apricot Ham

1 (6 to 8 pound) butt or shank ham	1
Whole cloves	
2 tablespoons dry mustard	30 mL
1¼ cups apricot jam	300 mL
1¼ cups packed light brown sugar	300 mL

- Place ham, fat side up, in slow cooker. Stick lots of whole cloves on outside of ham.

- In bowl, combine mustard, jam and brown sugar and spread all over ham.

- Cover and cook on LOW for 5 to 6 hours.

Saucy Ham Loaf

Great with sweet and hot mustard recipe below

1 pound ground ham	500 g
½ pound ground beef	250 g
½ pound ground pork	250 g
2 eggs, slightly beaten	2
1 cup Italian dry seasoned breadcrumbs	250 mL
1 (5 ounce) can evaporated milk	1 (140 g)
¼ cup chili sauce	60 mL
1 teaspoon each seasoned salt and pepper	5 mL

- Make foil handles for loaf using technique described on page 192.

- Combine all ingredients and form into loaf in vegetable cooking sprayed oblong slow cooker.

- Shape loaf so that neither end touches edge of cooker.

- Cover and cook on LOW for 6 to 7 hours.

- Serve with Sweet and Hot Mustard.

Sweet and Hot Mustard

Use on Ham Loaf or ham sandwiches.

4 ounces dry mustard	125 g
1 cup vinegar	250 mL
3 eggs, beaten	3
1 cup sugar	250 mL

- Mix mustard and vinegar until smooth and let stand overnight.

- Add eggs and sugar and cook in double boiler 8 to 10 minutes or until it coats the spoon.

- Cool and store in covered jars in refrigerator. Serve with Ham Loaf .

Ham Loaf
Great for leftover ham

1½ pounds cooked ground ham	500 to 750 g
1 pound ground turkey	500 g
2 eggs	2
1 cup seasoned breadcrumbs	250 mL
2 teaspoons chicken seasoning	10 mL

- In bowl, combine ground ham, ground turkey, eggs, seasoned breadcrumbs and 2 teaspoons (10 mL) chicken seasoning and mix well.

- Use hands to pick up loaf mixture and shape into short, fat loaf that will fit into oblong slow cooker.

- Cover and cook on LOW for 4 to 5 hours.

- Serve with Cherry Sauce for Ham Loaf.

Cherry Sauce for Ham Loaf

1 cup cherry preserves	250 mL
2 tablespoons cider vinegar	30 mL
Scant ⅛ teaspoon ground cloves	.5 mL
Scant ⅛ teaspoon ground cinnamon	.5 mL

- Place cherry preserves, vinegar and spices in saucepan and heat. Serve over slices of ham loaf.

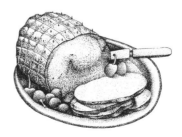

Ham and Potato Dish

4 large baking potatoes	4
3 cups cubed leftover ham	750 mL
1 (10 ounce) box frozen whole kernel corn, drained	1 (284 g)
1 (10 ounce) package frozen Seasoning Blend onions and peppers, thawed	1 (284 g)
1 teaspoon seasoned salt	5 mL
2 (10 ounce) cans fiesta nacho cheese soup	2 (284 g)
½ cup milk	125 mL
1 (3 ounce) can fried onion rings	1 (85 g)

- Cut potatoes into 1-inch cubes.

- In slow cooker combine potatoes, ham, corn, onions and peppers, seasoned salt, cheese soup and milk and stir to mix well.

- Cover and cook on LOW for 5 to 6 hours or until potatoes are tender.

- When ready to serve, sprinkle onions over top.

Ben's Ham and Rice

1 (6.7 ounce) box brown and wild rice, mushroom recipe	1 (193 g)
3 to 4 cups chopped or cubed, cooked ham	750 mL to 1 L
1 (4 ounce) can sliced mushrooms, drained	1 (125 g)
1 (10 ounce) package frozen green peas	1 (284 g)
2 cups chopped celery	500 mL

- In 4 to 5-quart (5 L) slow cooker, combine rice, seasoning packet, ham, mushrooms, peas, celery plus 2⅔ cups (675 mL) water. Stir to mix well.

- Cover and cook on LOW for 2 to 4 hours.

Creamy Potatoes and Ham

5 medium potatoes, peeled, sliced, divided	5
1 teaspoon seasoned salt, divided	5 mL
1 onion, chopped, divided	1
2 cups cooked, cubed ham, divided	500 mL
1 (8 ounce) package cubed processed cheese, divided	1 (225 g)
1 (10 ounce) can broccoli cheese soup	1 (284 g)
¼ cup milk	50 mL

- In slow cooker, layer half each of potatoes, seasoned salt, onion, ham and cheese and repeat layer.

- In bowl, combine soup and milk until fairly smooth.

- Cover and cook on HIGH for 1 hour.

- Reduce heat to LOW and cook for 6 to 7 hours.

Creamed Ham with Spaghetti

2 (10 ounce) cans cream of mushroom soup with roasted garlic	2 (284 g)
1 cup sliced fresh mushrooms	250 mL
2 to 2½ cups cooked, cubed ham	500 to 625 mL
1 (5 ounce) can evaporated milk	1 (140 g)
1 (7 ounce) box ready-cut spaghetti	1 (193 g)

- In slow cooker, combine soups, mushrooms, ham, evaporated milk and some salt and pepper.

- Cover and cook on LOW for 2 hours.

- In saucepan, cook spaghetti and drain. Add spaghetti to slow cooker and toss to coat.

Ham to the Rescue

2½ cups ground, cooked ham	625 mL
⅔ cup crushed white cheddar Cheeze-Its crackers	175 mL
1 large egg	1
⅓ cup chili sauce	75 mL
4 medium potatoes, peeled, sliced	4
1 green bell pepper, julienned	1
1 (8 ounce) package shredded cheddar-jack cheese	1 (225 g)
1 (5 ounce) can evaporated milk	1 (140 g)
1 teaspoon seasoned salt	5 mL

- In bowl, combine ham, crushed Cheeze-Its, egg and chili sauce and mix well.

- With hands, shape ham mixture into 6 patties and set aside.

- In skillet, saute potatoes in a little oil, turn several times to brown lightly on both sides and place potatoes and bell pepper in bottom of 6-quart (6 L) slow cooker.

- In another bowl, combine cheese, evaporated milk and seasoned salt and pour over potatoes.

- Place ham patties over potatoes.

- Cover and cook on LOW for 3 to 4 hours.

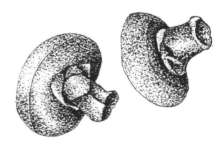

Sweet and Sour Sausage Links

2 (16 ounce) packages miniature smoked sausage links	1 (454 g)
¾ cup chili sauce	175 mL
1 cup packed brown sugar	250 mL
¼ cup prepared horseradish	60 mL

- Place sausages in 4-quart (4 L) slow cooker.

- Combine chili sauce, brown sugar and horseradish and pour over sausages.

- Cover and cook on LOW for 4 hours.

Tip: This can be served as an appetizer or served over hot cooked rice.

Tortellini Italian-Style

2 pounds bulk Italian sausage	1 kg
1 (15 ounce) carton refrigerated marinara sauce	1 (438 g)
2 cups sliced fresh mushrooms, sliced	500 mL
1 (15 ounce) cans Italian stewed tomatoes	1 (438 g)
1 (9 ounce) package refrigerated cheese tortellini	1 (240 g)
1½ cups shredded mozzarella cheese	375 mL

- Brown and cook Italian sausage about 10 to 15 minutes and drain.

- In 5-quart (5 L) slow cooker sprayed with vegetable cooking spray, combine sausage, marinara sauce, mushrooms and tomatoes.

- Cover and cook on LOW 6 to 7 hours.

- Stir in tortellini and sprinkle with cheese.

- Cover and cook on HIGH about 15 minutes or until tortellini is tender.

Sausage and Beans

1 (1 pound) fully cooked smoked, link sausage	1 (500 g)
2 (15 ounce) cans baked beans	2 (438 g)
1 (15 ounce) can great northern beans, drained	1 (438 g)
1 (15 ounce) can pinto beans, drained	1 (438 g)
½ cup chili sauce	125 mL
⅔ cup packed brown sugar	175 mL
1 tablespoon worcestershire sauce	15 mL

- Cut link sausage into 1-inch slices.

- In slow cooker, layer sausage and beans.

- Combine chili sauce, brown sugar, a little black pepper and worchestershire and pour over beans and sausage.

- Cover and cook on LOW for 4 hours. Stir before serving.

Sauerkraut and Bratwurst

1 (28 ounce) jar refrigerated sauerkraut	1 (800 g)
¾ cup beer	175 mL
1 tablespoon white wine worcestershire sauce	15 mL
1 (1.3 ounce) envelope dry onion soup mix	1 (32 g)
2 pounds precooked bratwurst	1 kg

- In 4 to 5-quart (5 L) slow cooker, combine sauerkraut, beer, worcestershire and onion soup mix and mix well.

- Cut bratwurst in diagonal slices and place on top of sauerkraut-beer mixture.

- Cover and cook on LOW for 5 to 6 hours or on HIGH for 2½ to 3 hours.

DESSERTS

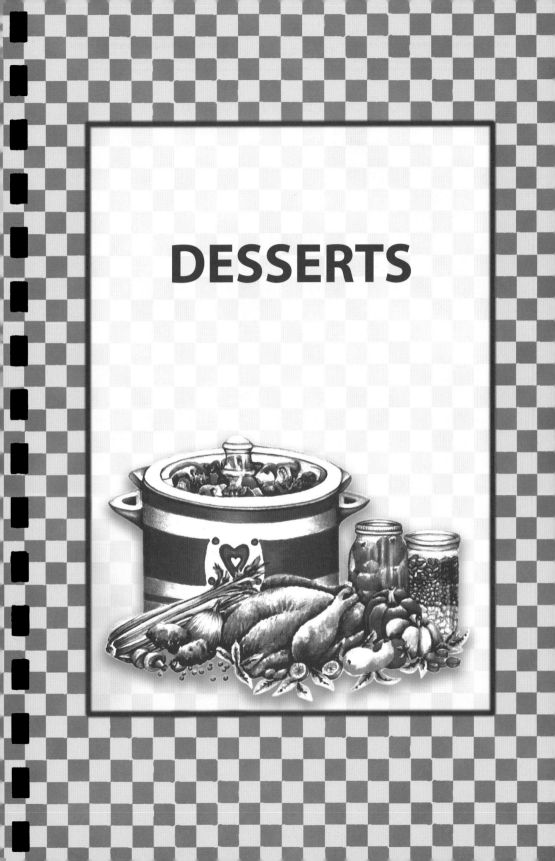

Delicious Bread Pudding

8 cups cubed leftover hot rolls, cinnamon rolls or cinnamon bread	2 L
2 cups milk	500 mL
4 large eggs	4
¾ cup sugar	175 mL
⅓ cup packed brown sugar	75 mL
¼ cup (½ stick)) butter, melted	60 mL
1 teaspoon vanilla extract	5 mL
¼ teaspoon nutmeg	1 mL
1 cup finely chopped pecans	250 mL

- Place cubed bread or rolls in slow cooker sprayed with vegetable cooking spray.

- In mixing bowl, combine, milk, eggs, both sugars, butter, vanilla and nutmeg and beat until smooth. Stir in pecans.

- Cover and cook on LOW for 3 hours.

- Serve with lemon sauce or whipped topping.

Baked Apples

4 or 5 large baking apples	4 or 5
1 tablespoon lemon juice	15 mL
1/3 cup dried craisins	75 mL
1/2 cup chopped pecans	125 mL
3/4 cup packed brown sugar	175 mL
1/2 teaspoon ground cinnamon	2 mL
1/4 cup (1/2 stick) butter, softened	60 mL

- Scoop out center of each apple and leave cavity about 1/2 inch from bottom.

- Peel top of apples down about 1 inch and brush lemon juice on peeled edges.

- In bowl, combine craisins, pecans, brown sugar, cinnamon and butter. Spoon mixture into apple cavities.

- Pour 1/2 cup (125 mL) water in oblong slow cooker and place apples on bottom.

- Cover and cook on LOW for 1 to 3 hours.

- Serve warm or room temperature drizzled with caramel ice cream topping.

Bread Pudding with Coconut and Nuts

1 cup sugar	250 mL
½ cup (1 stick) butter, softened	125 mL
1 teaspoon ground cinnamon	5 mL
4 eggs	4
3 cups white bread cubes	750 mL
⅓ cup flaked coconut	75 mL
⅓ cup chopped pecans	75 mL

- In mixing bowl, beat sugar, butter and cinnamon. Add eggs and beat well until it blends.

- Stir in bread, coconut and pecans. Pour into 4 to 5-quart (5 L) slow cooker.

- Cover and cook on LOW for 3 to 4 hours or on HIGH 1½ to 2 hours or until knife inserted into middle comes out clean.

Tip: Serve pudding warm with caramel ice cream topping, if desired.

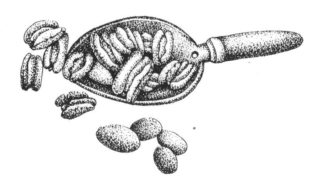

Butter-Baked Apples

6 large green baking apples	**6**
¼ cup (½ stick) butter, melted	**60 mL**
2 tablespoons lemon juice	**30 mL**
1 cup packed brown sugar	**250 mL**
1 teaspoon cinnamon	**5 mL**
½ teaspoon nutmeg	**2 mL**

- Peel, core, cut apples in half and place in slow cooker.

- Drizzle with lemon juice and butter. Sprinkle with sugar and spices.

- Cover and cook on LOW for 2½ to 3½ hours or on HIGH for 1½ to 2 hours.

- Serve with vanilla ice cream.

Fresh Peach Cobbler

1 cup sugar	250 mL
¾ cup baking mix	175 mL
2 eggs	2
2 teaspoons vanilla	10 mL
1 (5 ounce) can evaporated milk	1 (140 g)
2 tablespoons butter, melted	30 mL
3 large, ripe peaches, mashed	3

- Prepare slow cooker with vegetable cooking spray. In large bowl, combine sugar and baking mix, stir in eggs, vanilla, evaporated milk and butter and mix well.

- Fold in peaches and pour into slow cooker and stir well.

- Cover and cook on LOW for 6 to 8 hours or on HIGH for 3 to 4 hours.

- Serve warm with peach ice cream.

Peaches With Crunch

¾ cup uncooked old-fashioned oats	175 mL
⅔ cup packed brown sugar	150 mL
¾ cup granulated sugar	175 mL
½ cup baking mix	125 mL
½ teaspoon ground cinnamon	2 mL
2 (15 ounce) cans sliced peaches, well drained	2 (438 g)

- Lightly grease inside of 3 or 4-quart (4 L) slow cooker. In bowl, combine sugars, baking mix and cinnamon.

- Stir in drained peaches and spoon into slow cooker.

- Cover and cook on LOW for 4 to 5 hours. Serve in sherbet dishes.

DESSERTS

Pineapple-Rice Pudding

1 cup cooked white rice	250 mL
¾ cup sugar	175 mL
1 pint half-and-half cream	500 mL
1 tablespoon cornstarch	15 mL
3 eggs, beaten	3
1 teaspoon vanilla	5 mL
1 (15 ounce) can crushed pineapple, liquid reserved	1 (438 g)

- In mixing bowl combine rice, sugar and half-and-half and mix well.

- Stir in cornstarch, eggs, vanilla and pineapple.

- Pour into 4 to 5-quart (5 L) slow cooker coated with vegetable cooking spray.

- Cover and cook on LOW for 2 to 3 hours.

- When ready to serve, top each serving with toasted, chopped pecans as a special touch.

Surprise Dessert

1 (18 ounce) box spice cake mix	1 (510 g)
1 cup butterscotch chips	250 mL
4 eggs, slightly beaten	4
¾ cup oil	175 mL
1 (3.4 ounce) package butterscotch instant pudding mix	1 (100 g)
1 (8 ounce) carton sour cream	1 (225 g)
1 cup chopped pecans	250 mL

- Lightly grease inside of 4 or 5-quart (5 L) slow cooker.

- In large bowl, combine all ingredients and ¾ cup (175 mL) water. Pour into cooker.

- Cover and cook on LOW for 6 to 7 hours or on HIGH for 3 to 3½ hours.

- Serve hot or room temperature with butter-pecan ice cream.

Chocolate Delight

1 (18 ounce) box chocolate cake mix	1 (510 g)
1 (8 ounce) carton sour cream	1 (225 g)
4 eggs	4
¾ cup oil	175 mL
1 (3.4 ounce) box instant chocolate pudding mix	1 (100 g)
¾ cup chopped pecans	175 mL

- Prepare sides and bottom of slow cooker with vegetable cooking spray.

- In bowl mix cake mix, sour cream, eggs, oil, pudding mix, pecans and 1 cup (250 mL) water. Pour into slow cooker.

- Cover and cook on LOW for 6 to 8 hours. Serve hot or warm with vanilla ice cream.

Chocolate Fondue
Use the slow cooker as a fondue pot.

2 (7 ounce) chocolate bars, chopped	2 (193 g)
4 ounces white chocolate bar, chopped	1 (125 g)
1 (7 ounce) jar marshmallow creme	1 (193 g)
¾ cup half-and-half cream	175 mL
½ cup slivered almonds, chopped, toasted	125 mL
¼ cup amaretto	60 mL
Pound cake	

- In small slow cooker sprayed with vegetable cooking spray, combine broken chocolate bars, chopped white chocolate bar, marshmallow creme, half-and-half and almonds.

- Cover and cook on LOW for about 2 hours or until chocolates melt.

- Stir to mix well and fold in amaretto.

TIP: Use the slow cooker as a fondue pot or transfer chocolate mixture to a fondue pot. Cut pound cake into small squares and use to dip into fondue.

Cran-Apples for Pound Cake

1 (6 ounce) package dried apples	1 (170 g)
½ cup craisins	125 mL
3 cups cranberry juice cocktail	750 mL
¾ cup packed brown sugar	175 mL
2 cinnamon sticks, halved	2

- Spray 3 to 4-quart (4 L) slow cooker and add apples, craisins, juice, brown sugar and cinnamon sticks.

- Cover and cook on LOW for 4 to 5 hours or until liquid absorbs and fruit is tender.

- Serve warm, at room temperature or chilled over slices of pound cake or vanilla ice cream.

Fruit Sauce

8 cups fresh fruit, thinly sliced (peaches, pears, apples, apricots, etc.)	2 L
1 cup orange juice	250 mL
⅓ cup packed brown sugar	75 mL
⅓ cup granulated sugar	75 mL
2 tablespoons quick-cooking tapioca	30 mL
1 teaspoon grated fresh ginger	5 mL
⅔ cup dried cranberries or cherries	150 mL

- In 4-quart (4 L) slow cooker combine fruit, juice, sugars, tapioca and ginger.

- Cover and cook on LOW for 4 hours.

- Add cranberries or cherries and mix well. Cover and let stand for 10 to 15 minutes.

- To serve, spoon over slices of pound cake or ice cream.

Magnificent Fudge

2 (16 ounce) jars slightly salted, dry roasted peanuts	2 (454 g)
1 (12 ounce) package semi-sweet chocolate chips	1 (355 g)
1 (4 ounce) bar German chocolate, broken	1 (125 g)
2 (24 ounce) packages white chocolate bark or	2 (640 g)
(3 pounds) almond bark, chopped	1.5 kg

- Place peanuts in 5-quart (5 L) slow cooker sprayed with vegetable cooking spray. In layers, add chocolate chips, German chocolate and white chocolate bark.

- Cover and cook on LOW for 3 hours without removing lid.

- When candy cooks 3 hours, remove lid, stir and cool in covered slow cooker.

- Stir again and drop by teaspoon onto wax paper.

  TIP: For darker fudge, use 1 white bark and 1 dark bark.
  DO NOT STIR.

INDEX

COOKBOOKS PUBLISHED
BY COOKBOOK RESOURCES, LLC

Cooking With 5 Ingredients
The Ultimate Cooking With 4 Ingredients
The Best of Cooking With 3 Ingredients
Easy Gourmet Cooking With 5 Ingredients
Healthy Cooking With 4 Ingredients
Easy Slow Cooker Cookbook
Easy Dessert Cooking With 5 Ingredients
Quick Fixes With Mixes
Casseroles To The Rescue
Kitchen Keepsakes/More Kitchen Keepsakes
Mother's Recipes
Recipe Keepsakes
Cookie Dough Secrets
Gifts For The Cookie Jar
Cookbook 25 Years
Pass The Plate
Texas Longhorn Cookbook
Mealtimes and Memories
Holiday Treats
Homecoming
Cookin' With Will Rogers
Best of Lone Star Legacy Cookbook
Little Taste of Texas
Little Taste of Texas II
Southwest Sizzler
Southwest Ole
Classroom Treats
Leaving Home

www.cookbookresources.com

To Order **Easy Slow Cooker Cookbook:**

Please send_____copies @ $16.95 (U.S.) each $_____

Plus postage/handling @$6.00 each $_____

Texas residents add sales tax @ $1.23 each $_____

Check or Credit Card (Canada-credit card only) TOTAL $_____

Charge to my ❑ **VISA** or ❑ **MasterCard**

Account #_____

Expiration Date_____

Signature_____

Name_____

Address_____

City_____State_____Zip_____

Phone (day)_____ (night)_____

Mail or Call:
Cookbook Resources
541 Doubletree Dr.
Highland Village, Texas 75077
Toll Free (866) 229-2665
(972) 317-6404 Fax
www.cookbookresources.com

— —

To Order **Easy Slow Cooker Cookbook:**

Please send_____copies @ $16.95 (U.S.) each $_____

Plus postage/handling @$6.00 each $_____

Texas residents add sales tax @ $1.23 each $_____

Check or Credit Card (Canada-credit card only) TOTAL $_____

Charge to my ❑ **VISA** or ❑ **MasterCard**

Account #_____

Expiration Date_____

Signature_____

Name_____

Address_____

City_____State_____Zip_____

Phone (day)_____ (night)_____

Mail or Call:
Cookbook Resources
541 Doubletree Dr.
Highland Village, Texas 75077
Toll Free (866) 229-2665
(972) 317-6404 Fax
www.cookbookresources.com